THE MYSTIC MASTERS SPEAK!

THE MYSTIC MASTERS SPEAK!

A Treasury of Cosmic Wisdom

by
VERNON HOWARD

NEW LIFE FOUNDATION
Pine, Arizona 85544

(520) 476-3224
Web: www.anewlife.org
E-mail: info@anewlife.org

First published 1974
Second Impression 1976
Third Printing 1981
Fourth Printing 1994

ISBN 0-911203-23-0

FOR INFORMATION ON CLASSES, BOOKS,
TAPES AND VIDEO CASSETTES, WRITE:
NEW LIFE
PO BOX 2230
PINE, ARIZONA 85544

Contents

Five Programmes for a Rich Use of this Book

This book is for anyone who wants to escape from the trap. There *is* a way out. And you can find it. I assure you of this.

This book contains the concentrated wisdom of the ages. In this power-packed volume are all the answers you need for winning a New Life. Its solutions are simple, accurate, helpful. Here are the authentic answers to questions which have haunted man throughout the ages. It shows you how to abolish fear and loneliness, what to do about painful problems with other people, how to achieve ease, confidence, and a self-independence beyond your fondest dreams.

As you read, remember that the mystic path is unique, different. It is precisely this difference that makes it work for you. Have your old and usual ways uplifted you? If not, you can see the pleasant necessity of this totally fresh method. You see, the mystics whom you will meet are the most practical men on earth. They have no interest in fancy words; they simply and directly invite, 'Come, let me show you how to be an entirely new person.'

So be cheerfully willing to explore this fascinating world of the unknown. Let go of the past completely — it has done nothing for you. Desire to rise above your present self. Explore with an interested and alert mind, for that is what turns everything into gold.

As an extra value, you will find that some of these sets of questions and answers form a continued conversation for a while, just as if you were speaking back and forth with these great teachers.

Here are your five self-enriching programmes:

Programme 1: After your first reading of this book, practise random reading. The advantage of this volume is the ease with which you can pick it up and start reading anywhere. So open it when you have a few minutes at lunch, or between home projects. These short refreshments keep you inspired.

Programme 2: Join or form a study group. Great gain can be made when a number of earnest people come together for self-development. Large or small groups can meet in home, office, or church. The leader can read a page or two, then direct the discussion.

Programme 3: Write down the numbers of your favourite answers. There is a healthy reason why you received special impressions from them. Write them out on separate slips of paper and carry them with you. Now, fully mine their gold by memorizing and reflecting upon them.

Programme 4: Note all the answers which cover a topic of special interest to you, or which cover a specific problem, for example, you may wish to know all about freedom from anxiety. Then, read all the answers to your topic in one reading session. This brightens your understanding, just as a tourist understands a French castle better by viewing it from all sides.

Programme 5: This is the most important programme of your life! *Work at seeing something much higher in these truths than appears to you at first glance.* Let them tell you their secret story. The power of these lofty truths wishes to contact you, and it can succeed as you make it welcome. And then, at last, you will *know.*

Perhaps you have asked, 'Can I really know the truth that sets me free?' The answer is, of course you can. And you can start right now. You see, when the mystic masters speak, they know what they are talking about. So join them, and you will hear and understand the secret story; you will know what life is all about, and you will be the commander of your own life.

VERNON HOWARD

1. The Practical Power of Mystic Principles

1.   Q: May I come right to the point? What are mystical studies all about? Are they practical? What will they do for us?

A: If you devote your time to study, you will avoid all the irksome things of life, and you will not long for the approach of night, being tired of the day, and you will not be a burden to yourself, and your company will be acceptable to others. (Seneca)

2.   Q: But do these lofty mystical principles help us in daily matters, such as the solving of problems and in the making of necessary decisions? Heavenly ideas have their place, but we need down-to-earth assistance.

A: The contemplation of celestial things will make a man both speak and think more sublimely and magnificently when he descends to human affairs. (Cicero)

3.   Q: What about the control of personal habits? Can these principles give us a new and a complete command over ourselves, including the removal of unwanted habits?

A: Even the food and drink necessary for restoration will lie outside the soul's attention, and not less the sexual appetite . . . it will turn upon the actual needs of nature and be entirely under control. (Plotinus)

4.   Q: I don't have any large personal problems, but am puzzled by life in general. For example, why are we here on earth, and what am I supposed to be doing with myself?

A: We are surrounded by a rich and fertile mystery.

May we not probe it, pry into it, employ ourselves about it, a little? (Thoreau)

5.   *Q*: Then there is a definite answer regarding the purpose of life?

A: To be what we are, and to become what we are capable of becoming, is the only aim of life. (Spinoza)

6.   *Q*: I have always yearned to simply be myself, but tell me, how does it contribute to personal happiness?

A: Resolve to be thyself; and know, that he who finds himself, loses his misery. (Arnold)

7.   *Q*: What will be the signs that we are solving these mysteries of life for ourselves?

A: To be happy, to possess eternal life, to be in God, to be saved — all these are the same. All alike mean the solution of the problem, the aim of existence. And happiness is cumulative, as misery may be. An eternal growth is an unchangeable peace, an ever more profounder depth of understanding, a possession constantly more intense and more spiritual with the joy of heaven — this is happiness. Happiness has no limits. (Amiel)

8.   *Q*: I want to work at self-transformation, but I have no confidence in my mental abilities to understand what I must do.

A: We can be men without being sages. Without spending our days in the study of morality, we possess at a cheaper rate a more certain guide through the immense and perplexing labyrinth of human opinions. It is not enough, however, that such a guide exists — it is necessary to know and follow her. (Rousseau)

9.   *Q*: What is this authentic guide?

A: Be a lamp unto yourself. (Buddha)

You are wiser than you think!

10.   *Q*: I would give anything to be sure that my fate is not forever fixed, that I can really break completely away from my present negative patterns and enter a new way.

A: A strict belief in fate is the worst of slavery, imposing upon our necks an everlasting lord and tyrant, who we stand in awe of night and day. (Epicuras)

11.   *Q*: Then change and elevation of both self and circumstance is truly possible?

A: Man is man, and master of his fate. (Tennyson)

12.   *Q*: In this world of rapid changes, all of us seem to be seeking something more secure and permanent. Will you please comment on this?

A: One truth discovered is immortal, and entitles its author to be so: for, like a new substance in nature, it cannot be destroyed. (Hazlitt)

13.   *Q*: But maybe only certain types of people are able to set off on the mystic path. Or maybe we can take it up only when we have enough money or leisure; when we are free of the demands of everyday life.

A: You think it is because I have an income which exempts me from your day-labour, that I waste (as you call it) my time in sun-gazing and star-gazing. You do not know me. If my debts, as they threaten, should consume what money I have, I should live just as I do now: I should eat worse food, and wear a coarser coat, and should wander in a potato patch instead of in the wood — but it is I, and not my twelve hundred dollars a year, that love God. (Emerson)

14.   *Q*: I am aware that we must make personal efforts, but I am not sure as to what they are.

A: Ask, and it shall be given you; seek, and ye shall find; knock, and it shall be opened unto you: for every one that asketh receiveth; and he that seeketh findeth; and to him that knocketh it shall be opened. (Jesus)

15.   Q: Feelings of inferiority have always prevented me from attempting to climb the mountain. I often think that I lack the necessary inner qualities.

A: On the other hand, we are often wiser than we fancy ourselves to be . . . In the great moments of life, when a man decides upon an important step, his action is directed not so much by any clear knowledge of the right thing to do, as by an inner impulse — you may almost call it intuition — proceeding from the deepest foundations of his being. (Schopenhauer)

16.   Q: But what if we have limited time for attending to the inner life?

A: One day, with life and heart, is more than time enough to find a world. (Lowell)

Your path to lasting delight

17.   Q: Sometimes I find myself letting go of the mad rush of daily duties to wonder about myself and my activities. Surely there is something higher for us than the usual pursuits of making money and raising families. Do other people also have this feeling of wonder?

A: But often in the world's most crowded streets, but often, in the din of strife, there rises an unspeakable desire after the knowledge of our buried life, a thirst to spend our fire and restless force in tracking out our true, original course; a longing to inquire into the mystery of this heart that beats so wild, so deep in us, to know whence our thoughts come and where they go. (Arnold)

18.   Q: Will you please supply an example of a practical esoteric truth which needs our sincere study in order to make its value our own value?

A: Without going out of doors, one may know the whole world; without looking out of the window, one may see the way of heaven. The further one travels, the less one may know. Thus it is that without moving you may know; without looking you shall see; without doing you shall succeed. (Lao-tse)

19. *Q*: I often feel enslaved by compulsive duties. I do them because I feel I *must* or *should* do them. Because of this, I am a whirlpool of resentment and guilt. Is it wrong to want to break out of this nightmare and to start living my own life?

A: I would have nobody to control me; I would be absolute ... Now, he that is absolute can do what he likes; he that can do what he likes can take his pleasure; he that can take his pleasure can be content; and he that can be content has no more to desire. So the matter is over, and come what will come, I am satisfied. (Cervantes)

20. *Q*: I have always had a timid and apologetic attitude towards other people, which I dislike. I am encouraged by everything you say, but I am still what I am.

A: I do not trouble my spirit to vindicate itself or be understood; I see that the elementary laws never apologize. (Whitman)

21. *Q*: So how can I set myself free?

A: Who has bound you? (Zen)

22. *Q*: I sense something very right and very reassuring about everything we have covered so far. Will you please explain this feeling?

A: These are not fictions of a visionary imagination, but sober truths, spoken by the word of God in scripture, and written and engraven in the book of every man's own nature. (Law)

23. *Q*: Most of us have false values of one kind or another. We need guidance in exchanging shallow activities for more profitable ones. Please suggest a method.

A: There is nothing so delightful as the hearing or the speaking of truth. For this reason, there is no conversation so agreeable as that of a man of integrity, who hears without any intention to betray, and speaks without any intention to deceive. (Plato)

24.   *Q*: Will authentic values become clearer to us as we watchfully proceed?

A: Evident as the sun at noon. (Carlyle)

The interesting discoveries you will make

25.   *Q*: Suppose we reach this state of inner unity. Does this mean that the people and circumstances that now disturb us can have no more influence on our peace of mind?

A: No matter where you place it, gold is gold. (Ramakrishna)

26.   *Q*: What results have been obtained by those people who have dived deeply into esoteric waters? I mean, have they found special rewards in this inner world?

A: It was my conviction that I could not do better than continue in that in which I was engaged,. . . in making the greatest progress I was able in the knowledge of truth . . . This method, from the time I began to apply it, has been to me the source of satisfaction so intense as to make me believe that a more perfect or more innocent occupation could not be enjoyed in this life. By its means, I daily discovered truths that appeared to me of great importance, and of which other men were generally ignorant. The arising satisfaction so occupied my mind that I was wholly indifferent to every other object. (Descartes)

27.   *Q*: What discovered truth would open the door to lasting self-contentment?

A: He is happy as well as great who needs neither to obey nor to command in order to be something. (Goethe)

28.   *Q*: Does the absorption of mystic principles provide a man with the endurance needed for going on to new successes?

A: No man could ever make him face about. (Bunyan)

29.   *Q*: To summarize at this point, why is it necessary for us to study these mystical and esoteric teachings?

A: The true sovereign of the world, who moulds the world like soft wax, according to his pleasure, is he who lovingly sees into the world. (Carlyle)

30.   *Q*: I am easily upset by unexpected events which force me to change my plans. It is more annoying than tragic, still, it is no way to go through the day. May I have your comment?

A: The man of inner life is easily aware of himself, since he is never totally absorbed in outward affairs. Therefore, his exterior occupations and necessary activities do not distract him, and he adjusts himself to things as they come. The man whose inner life is well-ordered, is not bothered by strange and troublesome ways of others. A man is blocked and distracted by such things only as he permits himself to be. (Kempis)

31.   *Q*: Why are these great principles not known and practised by mankind as a whole?

A: The secrets of life are not shown except to sympathy and likeness. (Emerson)

32.   *Q*: In other words, each person must eagerly want them for himself?

A: Dare to be wise! (Horace)

How your natural forces help you

33.   *Q*: Everything seems to depend upon the source we look to for help. What rule can we follow?

A: Set your affection on things above, not on things on the earth. (New Testament)

34.   *Q*: Why do we fail so often in our attempts to win what we want? Why do results so often turn out contrary to our desires?

A: We, ignorant of ourselves, beg often our own harms, which the wise powers deny us for our good; so find we profit by losing of our prayers. (Shakespeare)

35.   *Q*: Please explain what you mean by human ignorance.

   A: By closing the eyes and slumbering, and consenting to be deceived by shows, men establish and confirm their daily life of routine and habit everywhere, which still is built on purely illusory foundations. Children, who play life, discern its true law. (Thoreau)

36.   *Q*: How can we awaken our natural powers and turn them to practical use?

   A: The mason employed on the building of a house may be quite ignorant of its general design, or, at any rate, he may not keep it constantly in mind. So it is with man: in working through the days and hours of his life, he takes little thought of its character as a whole . . . It is only when we come to view our life as a connected whole that our character and capacities show themselves in their true light; that we see how, in particular instances, some happy inspiration, as it were, led us to choose the only true path out of a thousand which might have brought us to ruin. (Schopenhauer)

37.   *Q*: Then it is correct to say that all wisdom is really self-wisdom?

   A: The kingdom of heaven is within. (Jesus)

38.   *Q*: I believe I understand this, but let me review. If we work and solve the mysteries of ourselves, we solve all other mysteries?

   A: As a man-of-war that sails through the sea, so this earth that sails through the air. We mortals are all on board a fast-sailing, never-sinking world-frigate, of which God was the ship-wright . . . Thus sailing with sealed orders, we ourselves are the repositories of the secret packet, whose mysterious contents we long to learn. There are no mysteries out of ourselves. (Melville)

39.   *Q*: No matter how hard I try to shake it off, a deep feeling of loneliness clings to me. I was told that mysticism has a new and workable solution to this problem, but I wonder whether I will be able to grasp it.

A : An heir finds the title-deeds of his house. Will he say, 'Perhaps they are forged?', and neglect to examine them? (Pascal)

40.   *Q*: How can we aid our own self-work?

A : Patience is powerful. (Longfellow)

A technique for pleasant living

41.   *Q*: What healthy changes will come to us as a result of acquiring information of a mystical nature?

A : From this kind of knowledge arises the most perfect satisfaction and contentment. (Spinoza)

42.   *Q*: I would like to use my mind for the specific purpose of avoiding hurt feelings when dealing with other people. How can I do this, for example, when I am criticized or slandered by someone?

A : Say nothing more to yourself than what the first appearances report. Suppose that it has been reported to you that a certain person speaks ill of you. This has been reported, but that you have been injured has not been reported . . . Thus then always abide by the first appearances, and add nothing yourself from within, and then nothing hurtful happens to you. (Aurelius)

43.   *Q*: What if we make foolish mistakes along the spiritual path?

A : I will go a thousand leagues in falsehood, that one step of the journey may be true. (Sufism)

44.   *Q*: Why do we fail to learn from our mistakes?

A : The fox condemns the trap, not himself. (Blake)

45.   *Q*: Speaking of mistakes and illusions, Shakespeare said that nothing is what it seems. Does this apply to human friendships?

A : What men have given the name of friendship to is

nothing but an alliance, a reciprocal accommodation of interests, an exchange of good offices; in fact, it is nothing but a system of traffic, in which self-love always proposes to itself some advantage. (La Rochefoucauld)

46.   *Q*: What simple rule can we rely upon for right behaviour at all times under all circumstances?

A: What is rational is real, and what is real is rational. (Hegel)

47.   *Q*: I am attracted to esoteric teachings because they point the way back to the simple and natural life. Will you please supply a technique for recovering naturalness?

A: Be neither the slave of your impulses and sensations of the moment, nor of an abstract and general plan; be open to what life brings from within and without, and welcome the unforeseen, and give to your life unity, and bring the unforeseen within the lines of your plan. Let what is natural in you raise itself to the level of the spiritual, and let the spiritual become once more natural. Thus will your development be harmonious. (Amiel)

48.   *Q*: People chatter so much about inner freedom, but few seem to really possess it. How can we start to understand the true meaning of self-liberty?

A: The wish to untie, through understanding of their true nature, the chains of selfishness and sensuality — this is the yearning for freedom. (Shankara)

49.   *Q*: I sense how practical all this really is, but hope it is a sunny path as well.

A: Cheerful, and yet profound, like an October afternoon. (Nietzsche)

50.   *Q*: No longer do I believe in what human beings carelessly label as love, however, authentic love must have a part in mystical wisdom. What is an elementary lesson?

A: Love is ever the beginning of knowledge, as fire is of light. (Carlyle)

Your stream of power and wisdom

51. *Q*: I am frustrated by my failure to attain my financial goals. What particular knowledge do I need?

A: Condition, circumstance, is not the thing; bliss is the same in subject or in king. (Pope)

52. *Q*: I have a strong wish to live in this kind of calm happiness, so could you be more specific about its attainment? How is it possible to banish strain and pressure in business matters?

A: A little consideration of what takes place around us every day would show us that a higher law than that of our will regulates events; that our painful labours are unnecessary and fruitless; that only in our easy, simple, spontaneous action are we strong . . . Place yourself in the middle of the stream of power and wisdom which animates all whom it floats, and you are without effort impelled to truth, to right, and a perfect contentment. (Emerson)

53. *Q*: If a man floated in the very centre of this stream of truth he would be a king!

A: Let him regain his Kingdom! (Bhagavad-Gita)

54. *Q*: We now have the facts, but need a method for making them part of our lives.

A: Let us put the ideas of our mind, just as we put things of the laboratory, to the test of experience. (Locke)

55. *Q*: Several of us in town have formed a study group for weekly exploration of mystic and esoteric principles. May we have a helpful idea for our first discussion?

A: True religion is the establishment by man of such a relationship to the Infinite Life around him, which, while connecting his life with Infinite Life, and directing his actions, is also in agreement with his reason and with human knowledge. (Tolstoy)

56.   *Q*: I want to be a winner in life, but I don't really understand what it means to win.

A: Self-conquest is the greatest of victories. (Plato)

57.   *Q*: What if we find difficulty in understanding what we must do?

A: Truth makes all things plain. (Shakespeare)

58.   *Q*: I am curious about a particular point about the various schools of mysticism, such as Taoism, Zen, and Sufism. They were founded in different places and ages, yet all teach the same basic principles.

A: There is one river of truth, which receives tributaries from every side. (Clement)

59.   *Q*: May we have some general rules for psychic success?

A: These are the stages through which we have to pass, and all those who persevere will succeed. Give up all argumentation and other distractions. Is there anything in this dry intellectual jargon? It only throws the mind off its balance and disturbs it. These things have to be realized. Will talking do that? So give up all vain talk. Read only those books which have been written by persons who have had realization. (Vivekananda)

60.   *Q*: How does this procedure bring good results?

A: People, generally, are not aware of the ease of mind there is in knowing where they are, and where they are going. The sensation of being lost is a keen distress. (Wallace)

How to maintain perfect poise

61.   *Q*: I believe you teach the existence 'of something which is totally different from the thousands of competing and contradictory opinions about life.

A: There are not different truths in the world, for truth is one and the same at all times and in every place. (Buddhism)

62.   Q: Are right and constructive thoughts always available to us?

A: As you grow ready for it, somewhere or other you will find what is needful for you in a book or a friend, or, best of all, in your own thoughts – the eternal thought speaking in your thought. (MacDonald)

63.   Q: What is the mystical definition of greatness?

A: He that is slow to anger is better than the mighty; and he that ruleth his spirit than he that taketh a city. (Old Testament)

64.   Q: Why do unhappy people fail to profit by listening to those who have superior spiritual insight?

A: We think few people sensible except those who are of our own opinion. (La Rochefoucauld)

65.   Q: In order to act, man needs some sort of motivation. What can light a fire under us to make us move towards the true life?

A: I appeal to nothing but the state of your own hearts and consciences, to prove the necessity of your embracing this mystery of divine love. (Law)

66.   Q: After searching for the answers to life for a long time, I have at least one solid conviction – organized society knows nothing. For example, I recently attended a meeting for the promotion of world peace – and the people spent most of their time fighting among themselves!

A: Take another example – a roomful of guests in full dress, being received with great ceremony. You could almost believe that this is a noble and distinguished company; but, as a matter of fact, it is compulsion, pain and boredom who are the real guests. For where many are invited, it is a rabble – even if they all wear stars. Really good society is everywhere of necessity very small. In brilliant festivals and noisy entertainments, there is always, at bottom, a sense of emptiness prevalent. A false tone is there. (Schopenhauer)

67.   *Q*: How can we retain our integrity and our poise when surrounded by such social falseness?

A: To live in the presence of great truths and eternal laws — that is what keeps a man patient when the world ignores him, and calm and unspoiled when the world praises him. (Balzac)

68.   *Q*: I am attracted by the idea of discovering new cosmic worlds which are now beyond my inner sight. How can I best apply myself?

A: Thinkers are as scarce as gold, but he whose thoughts embrace all his subject, pursues it persistently and is fearless of consequences, is a diamond of enormous size. (Lavater)

69.   *Q*: As all the great philosophers and religious teachers point out, most men live in an artificial happiness. I don't want to go along with it any longer.

A: Freedom has a thousand charms to show, that slaves, however contented, never know. (Cowper)

70.   *Q*: That is the message I have wanted to hear for many years.

A: Why not, then, take steps to be free? (Plautus)

A helpful summary of Chapter 1

a. Mystic principles are practical powers for daily use.
b. If you wish to change your life, you can succeed at it.
c. Make up your mind to live your own life!
d. The mystic way is one of delightful discoveries.
e. Receive these higher viewpoints as your own viewpoints.
f. Your natural forces are ready to assist you.
g. Work patiently with yourself every day.
h. You can dissolve all forms of frustration.
i. Permit these ideas to prove their value to you.
j. Here are the messages you have yearned to hear.

2. Your First Steps Towards a Richer Life

71.　*Q*: I am no longer satisfied with the shallow answers to life, which society offers so freely. The disasters we see all around us are evidence enough of society's failure. If it takes an independent search to break out of the desert, I am willing to make it. What must I know at the start?

A: If men would steadily observe realities only, and not allow themselves to be deluded, life, to compare it with such things as we know, would be like a fairy tale and the Arabian Nights' Entertainments. If we respected only what is inevitable and has a right to be, music and poetry would resound along the streets. (Thoreau)

72.　*Q*: So the chief cause of the human problem is human delusion?

A: Human life is thus only an endless illusion. Men deceive and flatter each other. No one speaks of us in our presence as he does when we are gone. Society is based on mutual hypocrisy. (Pascal)

73.　*Q*: And the solution?

A: If the doors of perception were cleansed, everything would appear to man as it is — infinite. (Blake)

74.　*Q*: How can we find proof of the rightness of this?

A: By far the best proof is experience. (Bacon)

75.　*Q*: But this seems to call for immense wisdom. The only thing I know is that I do not know!

A: The journey of a thousand miles begins with one step. (Lao-tse)

76.   *Q*: We have so many clamouring voices inside us which command us to do this or that. It is difficult to decide which ones speak for our true benefit.

A: Whenever conscience speaks with a divided, uncertain, and disputed voice, it is not yet the voice of God. Descend still deeper into yourself, until you hear nothing but a clear and undivided voice, a voice which does away with doubt and brings with it persuasion, light, and serenity. Happy, says the Apostle, are they who are at peace with themselves, and whose heart condemns them not in the part they take. (Amiel)

77.   *Q*: There was a time when I used to view life more clearly than I do at present. I don't know what happened, but somewhere along the way I must have fallen asleep.

A: To recover your life is in your power. Look at things again as you used to look at them, for in this consists the recovery of your life. (Aurelius)

78.   *Q*: What good results can be expected from self-awakening?

A: You shall know the truth, and the truth shall make you free. (Jesus)

79.   *Q*: What kind of truth will supply inner liberty?

A: You have not known what you are, you have slumbered upon yourself all your life . . . Whoever you are! Claim your own. (Whitman)

80.   *Q*: How do I start?

A: Know thyself. (Socrates)

81.   *Q*: Why do we fail to see ourselves as we really are?

A: We become so accustomed to disguise ourselves to others that at last we are disguised to ourselves. (La Rochefoucauld)

How self-study provides a sure cure

82.   Q: No doubt self-knowledge has its place, but doesn't it glue us to the very faulty self we want to escape? Shouldn't we keep our minds on more heavenly themes?

A: Know then thyself, presume not God to scan, the proper study of mankind is man. (Pope)

83.   Q: But what if we see negative and unpleasant things in ourselves? Won't this self-honesty discourage us from going on?

A: We think this state is terrible. We are wrong. It is there that we find peace and liberty. (Fénelon)

84.   Q: Because it leads to the cure?

A: Dare to be true. Nothing can need a lie. (Herbert)

85.   Q: I am afraid that most of us will have a lot of admitting to do!

A: A man should never be ashamed to own he has been in the wrong, which is but saying, in other words, that he is wiser today than he was yesterday. (Pope)

86.   Q: It has been said that knowledge is not the same thing as wisdom. Will you please explain the difference?

A: Knowledge and wisdom, far from being one, have oft-times no connection. Knowledge dwells in heads replete with thoughts of other men; wisdom in minds attentive to their own. (Cowper)

87.   Q: So our aim must be to go beyond mere head-knowledge?

A: He who learns the rules of wisdom, without conforming to them in his life, is like a man who labours in his field, but did not sow. (Saadi)

88.   Q: How can we build our desire for valuable self-knowledge?

A: Once you have tasted the secrets, you will have a strong desire to understand them. (Sufism)

89.   *Q*: I would like to understand the necessity of exploring these new principles. Perhaps all we need is a greater effort to make our established ideas work more efficiently.

A: What is the use of going right over the old track again? . . . You must make tracks unto the unknown. (Thoreau)

90.   *Q*: Are there frightening hazards in this exploration of the unknown?

A: There is always safety in valour. (Emerson)

91.   *Q*: I have followed many systems and have tried to have faith, but nothing changes. In what can I believe?

A: Dare to believe only in yourselves. (Nietzsche)

92.   *Q*: But we hear so much about the need for faith and trust and belief.

A: There is no need of words; believe in facts. (Ovid)

The intelligent course to self-success

93.   *Q*: What about those who claim to have the one and only way to man's deliverance?

A: Who dares to say that he alone has found the truth? (Longfellow)

94.   *Q*: Public leaders keep telling us that man will be happy just as soon as we devise and obey the right laws. What contribution can human laws make towards human happiness?

A: This legality therefore is not able to set thee free from thy burden. No man was as yet ever rid of his burden by him; no, nor ever is like to be . . . Believe me, there is nothing in all this noise. (Bunyan)

95.   *Q*: But human laws and rules do make changes in the way we live. Perhaps the answer is that they merely change our exterior behaviour, not our inner levels of happiness.

A: To imagine that five hundred men, drawn from every corner of the kingdom, will make a good law! Is it not a dreary joke, for which the people will sooner or later have to pay? They have a change of masters, that is all. (Balzac)

96.   *Q*: I can understand why a thorough knowledge of human nature and human ways is a necessary first step to self-freedom, but I do have a question. What will happen to us if we are left without the strength of organized society? What other way is there?

A: It is this, let me tell you . . . the strongest man in the world is he who stands most alone. (Ibsen)

97.   *Q*: It is interesting how we always come back to the basic fact that we must rely upon ourselves only, not upon those who claim to have the answers.

A: The eagle never lost so much time as when he submitted to learn of the crow. (Blake)

98.   *Q*: It is a relief to have my suspicions about deceitful human nature confirmed by those who see deeply into it. What practical procedure should we now follow?

A: You will see that, in dealing with fools and blockheads, there is only one way of showing your intelligence – by having nothing to do with them. That means, of course, that when you go into society, you may now and then feel like a good dancer who gets an invitation to a ball, and on arriving, finds that everyone is lame – with whom is he to dance? (Schopenhauer)

99.   *Q*: So what is the right and intelligent course of action for us when it comes to our own self-deliverance?

A: When you travel to the Celestial City, carry no letters of introduction. When you knock, ask to see God – none of the servants. (Thoreau)

Here is your pearl of great price

100. Q: Where can we find evidence that we are on the right track at last?

A: The spiritual life is as much its own proof as the natural life, and needs no outward or foreign thing to bear witness to it. (Law)

101. Q: Mysticism teaches that obstacles to our self-renewal exist only in our misunderstanding mind. Will you please discuss this?

A: If you wish to maintain a will conformable to nature, you have every security, every facility, you have no troubles. If you wish to maintain what is in your own power and is naturally free, and if you are content with these, what else do you care for? For who is the master of such things? Who can take them away? If you choose to be modest and faithful, who shall not allow you to be so? (Epictetus)

102. Q: What specific instruction will help us to win the kind of a self with whom we can live in peace?

A: Practise right view, right aim, right speech, right action, right living, right effort, right mindfulness, right meditation. (Buddha)

103. Q: What about the time factor? Is the search a long one?

A: Every day to a wise man is a new life. (Seneca)

104. Q: What is the nature of this new life towards which we are heading?

A: Do not require a description of the countries towards which you sail. The description does not describe them to you, and tomorrow you will arrive there and know them by inhabiting them. (Emerson)

105. Q: I am unacquainted with other people who are also interested in esoteric self-development. Is it possible to make progress by working alone?

A: Had I been born on a desert island, or had never seen a human creature beside myself; had I never been informed of what had formerly happened in a certain corner of the world, I might yet have learned, by the exercise and cultivation of my reason, and by the proper use of the faculties God has given me, to know and to love Him . . . and to have properly discharged my duty here on earth. What can the knowledge of the learned man teach me more? (Rousseau)

106. *Q*: How can we increase our talents in spiritual matters?

A: The heights of ability consists in a thorough knowledge of the real value of things. (La Rochefoucauld)

107. *Q*: I am aware that we can receive these great truths only to the degree that we value them, so please supply a thought to remind us to value them above all else.

A: The kingdom of heaven is like unto a merchantman, seeking goodly pearls: who, when he had found one pearl of great price, went and sold all that he had, and bought it. (Jesus)

How to build genuine enthusiam

108. *Q*: I am quite enthusiastic about these mystical teachings, and wish to work on them as efficiently as possible. What can you suggest?

A: Always run in the short way, and the short way is the natural; accordingly, say and do everything in conformity with the soundest reason. For such a purpose frees a man from trouble and warfare and all artificiality. (Aurelius)

109. *Q*: And I can work at this in my own way?

A: Each mind has its own method. (Emerson)

110. *Q*: What is a good method for ending wasteful artificiality in ourselves?

A: He who would distinguish the true from the false must have a clear idea of what is true and false. (Spinoza)

111. *Q*: My conclusions are often faulty. What I assume is right often turns out wrong. I would like to hear of a first step for self-correction.

A: The best way to come to truth being to examine things as really they are, and not to conclude they are, as we fancy of ourselves, or have been taught by others to imagine. (Locke)

112. *Q*: Isn't it valuable to observe the falseness of people we meet, I mean, as long as we avoid self-righteousness?

A: There are false heroes and false devotees; and as true heroes never are the ones who make much noise about their deeds of honour, just so true devotees, whom we should follow, are not the ones who make so much vain show. What! Will you find no difference between hypocrisy and genuine devotion? (Molière)

113. *Q*: I want to walk towards inner newness, but it all seems so mysterious and difficult!

A: It is not far, it is within reach. Perhaps you have been on it since you were born and did not know. (Whitman)

114. *Q*: But perhaps this inner adventure may call for sacrifices we are hesitant to make.

A: Where Nature is sovereign, there is no need for austerity and self-denial. (Froude)

115. *Q*: The saddest word in my vocabulary is *confusion*. Sometimes I play the role of a man who knows exactly what he is doing, but I can't fool my own self. Will you please provide a first step for banishing confusion in general?

A: What comfort, what strength, what economy there is in *order* – material order, intellectual order, moral order. To know where one is going and what one wishes – this is order; to keep one's word and one's engagements – again

order; to have everything ready under one's hand, to be able
to dispose of all one's forces, and to have all one's means of
whatever kind under command — still order; to discipline
one's habits, one's efforts, one's wishes; to organize one's life,
to distribute one's time . . . all this belongs to and is included
in the word *order*. Order means light and peace, inward
liberty and free command over oneself; order is power.
(Amiel)

116. *Q*: We are urged to meditate upon these lofty
principles, but I have never been able to determine the nature
of authentic meditation.

A: The intentness of the soul on the pure Eternal —
that is right meditation. It is not the indulgence in fanciful
thinking. (Shankara)

Why a new nature is necessary

117. *Q*: What is the connection between our spiritual level
and the level of our happiness?

A: The most certain sign of wisdom is continual
cheerfulness; her state is like that of things in the regions
above the moon, always clear and serene. (Montaigne)

118. *Q*: I have noticed that all of the great teachers
emphasize the need for honestly observing and then abandoning our negative traits. I wonder why they give so much
attention to the losing of negative features, instead of
showing us how to acquire positive traits.

A: We lop away that bearing boughs may live.
(Shakespeare)

119. *Q*: It is strange how we resist the loss of those very
things that harm us.

A: So Nature deals with us, and takes away our
playthings one by one, and by the hand leads us to rest.
(Longfellow)

120. *Q*: Lately I have been thinking about the difference

between a surface reform of our character and the acquisition of a totally transformed nature. Why do esoteric teachings insist upon a completely new nature?

A: Of what use to make heroic vows of amendment, if the same old law-breaker is to keep them? (Emerson)

121. *Q*: By what method is this new nature acquired?

A: The realization of Truth is brought about by perception, and not in the least by ten millions of acts. (Shankara)

122. *Q*: And this new nature sets us free of old problems?

A: Free as an eagle. (Keats)

123. *Q*: This inner transformation makes perfect sense, but where does our duty towards others come in? Some may think it is self-centred to work on ourselves, instead of with and for others.

A: He who reforms himself has done more towards reforming the public than a crowd of noisy, impotent patriots. (Lavater)

124. *Q*: So this is why esotericism calls for personal change, rather than for social rearrangement?

A: For the outward world is but a glass, a represent-ation of the inward; and everything, and variety of things in temporal nature, must have its root or hidden cause in something that is more inward. (Law)

125. *Q*: May we have a first step towards building persist-ence along the mystic path?

A: Be not disgusted, nor discouraged, nor dissatisfied, if you do not succeed in doing everything according to right principles, but when you fail, return back again, and be content if the greater part of what you do is consistent with man's nature. Love this to which you return, and do not return to philosophy as if she were a master, but act like those who have tired eyes and apply a drenching with water.

Then you will not fail to obey reason, and you will repose in it. (Aurelius)

126. *Q:* I feel that I could advance much faster if I were free of certain people who are harmful to me. Is there some counsel to cover this problem?

A: Consider what your bondage is in the world. What do you not have to suffer to keep the esteem of those men whom you scorn? (Fénelon)

Where lasting happiness is found

127. *Q:* My main problem is my own contradictory attitudes. At the same time that I want to please myself, I also want to please others, so I often submit to their wishes.

A: Nearly all men are slaves for the same reason that the Spartans assigned for the servitude of the Persians — the inability to pronounce the word 'No'. To be able to speak that word and to live alone, are the only two means to preserve one's freedom and one's character. (Chamfort)

128. *Q:* So happiness can be found only in self-independence?

A: Even in the common affairs of life, in love, friendship, and marriage, how little security have we when we trust our happiness in the hands of others! (Hazlitt)

129. *Q:* It is getting clearer to me why self-understanding and spiritual knowledge must be highly valued by us.

A: Happy is the man that findeth wisdom, and the man that getteth understanding . . . She is more precious than rubies: and all things thou canst desire are not to be compared unto her. (Old Testament)

130. *Q:* What part does curiosity play in self-advancement?

A: There are different kinds of curiosity; one springs from interest, which makes us desire to know everything that may be profitable to us; another from pride, which springs from a desire to know what others do not know. (La Rochefoucauld)

131. *Q*: I am willing to change my mind if it becomes evident that I am wrong, but how can we guard against trading one wrong notion for a worse one?

A: A man should always have these two rules in readiness: the one, to do only whatever the reason of the ruling and legislating faculty may suggest . . . the other, to change his opinion, if some other person sets him right, and moves him from an opinion. But this change of opinion must proceed only from a certain persuasion, as of what is just or of common advantage, and the like, not because it appears pleasant or brings reputation. (Aurelius)

132. *Q*: I feel that I am standing in my own way. Might that be a correct analysis?

A: What is man's chief enemy? Each man is his own. (Anacharsis)

133. *Q*: This seems to knock out the complaints we have towards others.

A: The violence that others do to us is often less painful than violence we do to ourselves. (La Rochefoucauld)

134. *Q*: How can I strengthen both my interest and my effort in remaking my life with these practical programmes?

A: To love truth for truth's sake is the principal part of human perfection in this world, and the seed of all other virtues. (Locke)

135. *Q*: We now have some idea of what we must do to enrich ourselves, but what must we avoid doing?

A: Everything which compromises the future or destroys my inner liberty, which enslaves me to things or obliges me to be other than I could and ought to be . . . hurts me. (Amiel)

136. *Q*: We are so unaware of ourselves! We need something to correct us when we stray from the right path.

A: Nature brings us back to absolute truth whenever we wander. (Agassiz)

137. *Q*: I appreciate the encouragement offered by these principles, for there is certainly nothing encouraging in the offerings of the exterior world.

A: A few golden apples are rolled, and the world scrambles after them. You were never bound by laws, Nature never had a bond for you . . . We have placed ourselves in this net, and will have to get out . . . Never forget this is only a momentary state, and that we have to pass through it. (Vivekananda)

Take this leap to safety!

138. *Q*: How can we acquire the deep understanding which provides both inner and outer harmony?

A: Learn to distinguish between Self and Truth. Self is the cause of selfishness and the source of evil; Truth cleaves to no self; it is universal and leads to justice and righteousness. (Buddhism)

139. *Q*: How can I answer someone who says he wants freedom from his negative thoughts, but refuses to face and admit them?

A: No one can conquer an enemy without coming in sight of him. (Swedenborg)

140. *Q*: I am getting more conscious of how we carelessly permit other people to drain our psychic strength. Since we need to conserve our energies, will you please comment and advise?

A: If a man stands high in Nature's lists it is natural and inevitable that he should feel solitary. It will be an advantage to him if his surroundings do not interfere with this feeling; for if he has to see many other people who are not of like character with himself, they will exercise a disturbing influence upon him, adverse to his peace of mind; they will rob him, in fact, of himself, and give him nothing to compensate for the loss. (Schopenhauer)

141. Q: Sometimes an interesting challenge can arouse us to great effort. Please give us a challenge.

A: We are very near to greatness: one step and we are safe: can we not take the leap? (Emerson)

142. Q: The idea of returning to natural living has always had a great appeal to me. Also, I believe it is a basic teaching of Zen. What is the secret appeal of naturalness?

A: Nature never says one thing and wisdom another. (Juvenal)

143. Q: How does a knowledge of psychological or cosmic laws help us, and what is an example of a law we must understand?

A: Happy is he who has been able to learn the causes of things. (Virgil)

144. Q: Sometimes I feel utterly worthless.

A: There is a treasure in every person. (Sufism)

145. Q: So our task is to uncover this treasure, to realize that we had it all along?

A: Every man has within himself a continent of undiscovered character. Happy is he who proves to be the Columbus of his spirit. (Goethe)

146. Q: Where do the everyday virtues of goodness and kindness enter into our self-work? Will we spontaneously turn into nicer people?

A: You may, then, boldy declare that the highest good is singleness of mind, for where agreement and unity exist, there must the virtues be. It is the vices that are at war with each other. (Seneca)

147. Q: What advice do you have for helping us at the early stages of our mystical studies?

A: If we would put some slight stress on ourselves at the beginning, then afterwards we should be able to do all things with ease and joy. (Kempis)

148. Q: Please summarize our needed course of action.

A: Sleep no more! (Shakespeare)

Review these valuable points

a. As the mind becomes clearer, so does life.
b. Start right where you are to change your fortunes!
c. Self-honesty is a tremendous power in your favour.
d. Courageously plunge into new and different ideas.
e. You can become your own harbour of security.
f. Let self-elevation come through self-knowledge.
g. Orderly self-study will banish all confusion.
h. Your first duty is to self-harmony, not to society.
i. Learn to step out of your own way.
j. Our task is to awaken from psychic sleep.

3. How to Win New Control in Human Relations

149. Q: I always like to get the single most important fact about any subject and then give it my total attention and study. Will you therefore please state the single most important fact about understanding other people and having right relationships with them?

A: Would you know others? Read yourself — and learn! (Schiller)

150. Q: Please supply an example of this.

A: We are never more discontented with others than when we are discontented with ourselves. The consciousness of wrongdoing makes us irritable, and our heart in its cunning quarrels with what is outside it, in order that it may deafen the clamour within. (Amiel)

151. Q: What is the connection between the right use of our mental powers and harmonious human relations?

A: He that follows the advice of reason has a mind that is elevated above the reach of injury; that sits above the clouds, in a calm and quiet ether, and with a brave indifference hears the rolling thunders grumble and burst under his feet. (Scott)

152. Q: Where do we make a mistake in seeking happiness with other people?

A: We take less pains to be happy than to appear so. (La Rochefoucauld)

153. Q: I was once advised to never carelessly reveal any of my faults or weaknesses to others. Why?

A: Malice always aims where weakness can be injured. (Gracián)

154. *Q*: We are aware of how humanity likes to flatter itself on its wisdom and heroism, but how does an awakened man see it?

A: But man, proud man, drest in a little brief authority, most ignorant of what he's most assured, his glassy essence, like an angry ape, plays such fantastic tricks before high heaven as make the angels weep. (Shakespeare)

155. *Q*: What is the explanation of those rare moments between two people when all pretence and division falls away, and both quietly understand?

A: The beautiful attracts the beautiful. (Hunt)

156. *Q*: We are all so impatient and so frustrated in our dealings with each other. By what method can we show more gentleness and understanding?

A: The art of putting up with people may be learned by practising patience on inanimate objects, which, in virtue of some mechanical or general physical necessity, oppose a stubborn resistance to our freedom of action — a form of patience which is required every day. The patience thus gained may be applied to our dealings with men, by accustoming ourselves to regard their opposition, wherever we encounter it, as the inevitable outcome of their nature, which sets itself up against us according to the same rigid law of necessity which governs the resistance of inanimate objects. To become indignant at their conduct is as foolish as to be angry with a stone because it rolls into your path. (Schopenhauer)

How to avoid human traps

157. *Q*: Many of my actions in social relations have turned out less beneficial than expected, and have sometimes ended in disaster. How can we avoid getting mixed up with the wrong people?

A: Inasmuch as we neither seek nor shun any object except as our understanding represents it as either good or bad, all that is necessary to right action is right judgement . . . and the assurance of such an acquisition cannot fail to render us contented. (Descartes)

158. *Q*: We are always building something, always trying to create an existence which is higher and better and more tranquil. Yet with all this effort, everything remains the same, including our shaky state of happiness.

A: The difficulty is that we do not make a world of our own, but fall into institutions already made. (Emerson)

159. *Q*: We are told that obedience to our true and original nature results in carefree relations with other people, so I must have made a mistake somewhere. I believe that I live from my authentic self, yet I still make blunders with others.

A: The chief of our concerns is that of ourselves, yet how often have we not been told by the inner voice, that to pursue our own interests at the expense of others would be to do wrong! So we imagine that we are sometimes obeying the impulse of nature, but all the while we are resisting it. In listening to the voice of our senses, we turn a deaf ear to the dictates of our hearts. (Rousseau)

160. *Q*: What makes us so gullible that we repeatedly fall into traps set by others? What trickery should we watch for?

A: Self-interest speaks all sorts of tongues, and plays all sorts of roles, even that of disinterestedness. (La Rochefoucauld)

161. *Q*: What is the mystical method for remaining unharmed by the deceitfulness and slander of others?

A: If a man empties himself of himself, who can harm him? (Chuang-tse)

162. *Q*: I suppose that you mean we must empty ourselves of false values, like pride and self-righteousness. But how does this protect a man from the hostility of others?

A: Having nothing, nothing can he lose. (Shakespeare)

163. *Q*: Ordinary religion and psychology have a hard time defining human evil. What is the esoteric definition?

A: The only good is knowledge, and the only evil is ignorance. (Diogenes)

164. *Q*: Most people are really shy and frightened of each other. Is this a natural and necessary state, or an acquired false condition which can be corrected?

A: We are troubled only by the fears which we, and not nature, give ourselves. (Pascal)

Solving mankind's greatest problem

165. *Q*: Will you please explain man's fundamental problem, I mean, what is the cause of his confused and self-defeating ways?

A: The greatest part of mankind . . . may be said to be asleep, and that particular way of life which takes up each man's mind, thoughts, and actions, may be very well called his particular dream. This degree of vanity is equally visible in every form and order of life. The learned and the ignorant, the rich and the poor, are all in the same state of slumber. (Law)

166. *Q*: Do you mean that human beings actually live, work, play, marry, pass laws, fight wars – all in a state of psychic sleep, or illusion?

A: While they dream, they do not know that they are dreaming. (Lao-tse)

167. *Q*: It all makes sense, but it is shocking to realize that all our activities and virtues are nothing but gigantic stage performances.

A: Nothing is more terrible than active ignorance. (Goethe)

168. *Q*: For example?

A: The Puritans hated bear-baiting, not because it gave pain to the bear, but because it gave pleasure to the spectators. (Macaulay)

169. *Q*: I have suspected all this for a long time. If we are to get out of the woods, we need all the guidance we can get. Where can we start our self-awakening?

A: Judge not according to the appearances, but judge righteous judgment. (Jesus)

170. *Q*: What is righteous judgment?

A: To judge is to see clearly, to care for what is just and therefore to be impartial, more exactly, to be disinterested, more exactly still, to be impersonal. (Amiel)

171. *Q*: The evidence of man's self-defeating behaviour is too overwhelming to dismiss, but won't we find it upsetting or depressing to give it much attention?

A: If you come across any special trait of meanness or stupidity . . . you must be careful not to let it annoy or distress you, but to look upon it merely as an addition to your knowledge — a new fact to be considered in studying the character of humanity. Your attitude towards it should be that of the mineralogist who stumbles upon a very characteristic specimen of a mineral. (Schopenhauer)

172. *Q*: I have found that daily association with mystical teachings is by itself a reliable source of guidance through the world of people.

A: He that walks with wise men shall be wise. (Old Testament)

173. *Q*: I am part of a study group which meets on Tuesday evenings. We want to make the most of the session. Can you outline the best classroom attitude and action for each of us?

A: He who diligently attends, pointedly asks, calmly speaks, coolly answers, and ceases when he has no more to say, is in possession of some of the best requirements of conversation. (Lavater)

Be guided by cosmic principles

174. *Q*: How does an understanding of cosmic principles, like those taught by the mystics, help us in our human affairs?

A: He who knows the Tao is sure to be well acquainted with the principles that appear in the procedures of things. Acquainted with those principles, he is sure to understand how to regulate his actions in all kinds of circumstances. Having that understanding, he will not allow things to injure him. (Taoism)

175. *Q*: Does that apply to those times when we feel ourselves to be the helpless victims of circumstances and of other people? What cosmic principle covers this situation?

A: My true being, the essence of my nature, myself, remains inviolate and inaccessible to the world's attacks. (Amiel)

176. *Q*: What is a right and a mature attitude for starting our day?

A: Begin in the morning by saying to yourself, 'I shall meet with the busybody, the ungrateful, arrogant, deceitful, envious, unsocial. All these things happen to them because of their ignorance of what is good and evil . . . I cannot be injured by any of them.' (Aurelius)

177. *Q*: Is it true that we can use all uncomfortable conditions for gaining more valuable self-insight? If so, will you please show us how?

A: Your friends will tell you that they are sincere; your enemies are really so. Let your enemies' criticism be like a bitter medicine, to be used as a means of self-knowledge. (Schopenhauer)

178. *Q*: But perhaps I have wasted my powers for self-insight beyond recovery.

A: Of that which belongs to a man, he cannot rid himself, even though he were to throw it away. (Goethe)

179. *Q*: I know a woman who speaks quite rudely at times, but justifies it by calling herself a frank person. What is her particular problem?

A: We endeavour to make a virtue of the faults we are unwilling to correct. (La Rochefoucauld)

180. *Q*: Why is it such a shock and a disappointment when someone whom we like or admire suddenly reveals hidden badness?

A: It is foolish to be surprised when a fig tree produces figs. (Aurelius)

181. *Q*: I don't suppose it is wrong to mention our problems, at least some of them, to other people, but still it seems so pointless. I have noticed that many people actually enjoy hearing of another person's problem because it distracts them from their own. Please comment.

A: Our dependence upon God ought to be so entire and absolute that we should never think it necessary, in any kind of distress to seek out human consolations. (Kempis) .

182. *Q*: At times it seems difficult to put these principles into daily operation. I guess I need encouragement!

A: Choose always the way that seems right; however rough it may be. Practice will make it easy and pleasant. (Pythagoras)

The power of honest self-observation

183. *Q*: Since self-change is the only road to changed and happier relations with others, what is a common but wrong attitude we must banish in ourselves?

A: We are slow to believe those things which, if believed, would hurt our feelings. (Ovid)

184. *Q:* Could you please be specific about the need for noticing negative states in ourselves, as a first step towards dismissing them?

A: Who has not at one time or other felt a sourness, wrath, selfishness, envy and pride, which he could not tell what to do with, or how to bear, rising up in him without his consent, casting a blackness over all his thoughts, and then as suddenly going off again, either by the cheerfulness of the sun or air, or some agreeable accident, and again, at times, as suddenly returning upon him? Sufficient indications are these to every man that there is a dark guest within him . . . often lulled to sleep by worldly light and amusements. (Law)

185. *Q:* So self-observation and self-honesty are the way out of the cave?

A: This is the way thou must go. (Bunyan)

186. *Q:* People come into our lives and they exit from our lives. What basic thought can help us to experience these changes in the right way?

A: I have learned in whatsoever state I am, therewith to be content. (New Testament)

187. *Q:* I am in a position where I can freely give gifts and other benefits to various people, including my children. Sometimes I sense that I must not yield to some of their requests, which sets up a vague conflict in me. Can you explain this?

A: For this is the hardest of all; to close the open hand out of love. (Nietzsche)

188. *Q:* I am anxious and uncertain because I often do not know what to do in these complex human affairs.

A: What need is there of fear, since it is in your power to inquire what ought to be done? (Aurelius)

189. *Q:* What about the problem of making the right decisions? How can I know which decision is truly best?

A: If our eyes were opened, we should see it. (Boehme)

190. *Q*: I feel the need for certain people and for society in general, but at the same time I resent the obligations they place me under. Please comment.

A: How much easier it is to live in simplicity, than to be obligated to those who might enrich me. (Sufism)

191. *Q*: What do the mystics have to say about human humility? I am afraid I have some suspicions here.

A: Humility is often only a feigned submission, of which we make use to make others submissive. It is the trickery of pride which abases itself in order to exalt itself, and though it transforms itself in a thousand different ways, it is never better disguised and more capable of deceiving than when it conceals itself under the cloak of humility. (La Rochefoucauld)

Learn these facts about human nature

192. *Q*: What if a person commits a wrong, but says he is sorry about it afterwards. Should we not accept his remorse as fully genuine?

A: He will inevitably repeat the offence, or do something similar to it, should the occasion return, even though for the moment he is deep and sincere in his assurances of the contrary. There is nothing, absolutely nothing, that a man cannot forget, *except himself, his own character.* For character is incorrigible, because all a man's actions arise from an inward principle; he must always do the same thing under like circumstances, and he cannot do otherwise. (Schopenhauer)

193. *Q*: Then how can anyone change his basic nature from bad to good? What is man's way out of himself?

A: The great law of culture is: Let each become all that he was created capable of being; expand, if possible, to his full growth; resisting all impediments, casting off all foreign, especially all noxious adhesions, and show himself at length in his own shape and stature, be these what they may. (Carlyle)

194. Q: What can we do to make this a real experience in our lives?

A: Sickness is not cured by saying'Medicine', but by drinking it. So a man is not free by the name of the Eternal without discerning the Eternal. (Shankara)

195. Q: How would you describe genuine humility?

A: It costs us a great deal of trouble not to be of the same opinion as our self-love, and not be too ready to believe in the good taste of those who believe in our merits. (Amiel)

196. Q: Why do cruel people often win great prosperity and public honours, and how do they get away with their wickedness?

A: Does anyone do wrong? It is to himself that he does the wrong. (Aurelius)

197. Q: Then wickedness is its own punishment?

A: There is no greater punishment of evil than that it is dissatisfied with itself and its deeds. (Seneca)

198. Q: But what is the esoteric explanation for the huge success and fame of some people who are neither talented nor conscientious?

A: Fortune brings in some boats that are not steered. (Shakespeare)

199. Q: How does the law of cause and effect operate in our relations with other people?

A: We receive but what we give. (Coleridge)

200. Q: I am fascinated by a particular branch of that law. It states that the man who does good to himself will spontaneously do good to others, and that whoever harms

himself also hurts others. This proves absolutely that self-development must be our first development. Please comment on this principle.

A: You can depend upon no man, upon no friend, but on him who depends upon himself. Only he who acts beneficially towards himself will act so towards others. (Lavater)

201. *Q*: If we suspect that someone is concealing his real and his selfish motives from us, how can we discover them?

A: We endeavour to conceal our vices under the disguises of the opposite virtues. (Fielding)

How self-conquest brings peace

202. *Q*: Please supply a basic truth about love, I mean, about authentic love, not what people call love.

A: The deepest and most passionate love is that which survives the extinction of esteem. (Ouida)

203. *Q*: We have been taught that knowledge of what is truly right is already within us, and when awakened, we need no other authority. What is a specific instance of this?

A: The rule for doing unto others as you would wish them to do unto you, calls for no miraculous proof, neither does it require faith, because the rule is convincing in itself, both to reason and to human nature. (Tolstoy)

204. *Q*: What superior state of mind will be ours when we have completed our needed tasks?

A: I am quite my own master, agreeably lodged, perfectly easy in my circumstances. I am contented with my situation, and happy because I think myself so. (Le Sage)

205. *Q*: So self-conquest automatically includes conquest over our human circumstances, whatever they may be?

A: Such a man comes to tranquillity, and out of that tranquillity shall rise the end and healing of his earthly pains. (*Bhagavad-Gita*)

206. *Q*: But I cannot imagine any world other than the troublesome one I now inhabit!

A: There are more things in heaven and earth . . . than are dreamt of in your philosophy. (Shakespeare)

207. *Q*: The mystics state that there is a great difference between the man who publicly claims to be concerned for others, and the man who lives from the truth in a quiet and natural manner. Have I summarized this particular idea correctly?

A: The moral enthusiast, who in the maze of his subtleties, loses or despises the plain paths of honesty and duty, is on the brink of crimes. (Lavater)

208. *Q*: What special abilities does a mystical-minded man possess?

A: His eyes can read men's inmost hearts, and all the art of hypocrites cannot deceive him. HIs sharp discernment sees things clear and true. (Molière)

209. *Q*: And such a man possesses all those virtues and powers we have been discussing, such as deep cosmic knowledge and authentic compassion for wandering mankind?

A: Such men not only liberate themselves; they fill those they meet with a free mind. (Philo)

210. *Q*: There is far more anger and resentment between people than anyone likes to admit. What information can banish these harmful emotions?

A: A physician is not angry at the intemperance of a mad patient, nor does he take it ill to be insulted by a man in a fever. Just so, should a wise man treat all mankind as a physician treats a patient, and look upon it only as sick and irresponsible. (Seneca)

211. *Q*: I believe mysticism can be described as a system for *unlearning,* that is, we must cease to know so many wrong things.

A: Know not what you know. (Plautus)

The truth is always with you

212. *Q*: Is there a tactful and effective way to correct a person who is wrong but cannot see it?

A: When we wish to correct with advantage, and to show another that he errs, we must notice from what side he views the matter, for on that side it is usually true, and admit that truth to him, but reveal to him the side on which it is false. He is satisfied with that, for he sees that he was not mistaken, and that he only failed to see all sides. (Pascal)

213. *Q*: How can we tame the surrounding world?

A: It is good to tame the mind. (Buddhism)

214. *Q*: We are told we must adjust to society, but I am beginning to suspect this advice comes from the maladjusted. Certainly we must seek mental harmony and not try to adjust to hypnotized humanity.

A: It is a misfortune to have to manoeuvre one's heart as a general has to manoeuvre his army. (Smith)

215. *Q*: I often find myself in the conflict of wanting something and not wanting it at the same time, like trying to please someone while wishing I were free of him. Can I rise above this?

A: The heart is made to reconcile contradictions. (Hume)

216. *Q*: Then we can find instant relief from self-battling?

A: It is our prerogative as spiritual beings, that we can rise above the feeling of the moment, above all that is isolated and individual. (Caird)

217. *Q*: Can these ideas work to change us, even when we have little understanding of them, and even when part of us resists them? In other words, is the truth on our side, even when we are not on our own side?

START LIFE ALL OVER

DISCOVER A NEW WAY TO:

Solve problems • **Command events** • **Heal hurts** • **Stop stress**

Be at ease • **Have happy relations** • **End loneliness** • **Know true love**

It works! Over 8 million enthusiastic readers have been helped.

"I know of no one in life or literature who compares to Vernon Howard in enlightened understanding of human problems and solutions."

— Dr. Lynne Wooldridge

Please send me a FREE color catalog of Vernon Howard's life-healing books, booklets, MP3 CDs, DVDs, Blu-rays & much more.

NAME _____

ADDRESS _____

CITY _____ STATE _____ ZIP _____

Mail this card today or call (928) 476-3224 • www.anewlife.org

NEW LIFE FOUNDATION
PO BOX 2230
PINE AZ 85544

USA

A: No one can see these truths in the manner that I have presented them, without being in some degree inclined to believe them, and in some degree stirred up to act in conformity to them. (Law)

218. *Q*: Then there is at least a small part of us that always wants to know and do what is right?

A: Our minds possess by nature an insatiable desire to know the truth. (Cicero)

219. *Q*: How is a higher truth communicated to receptive minds?

A: The pure man . . . has the power of bringing it into a certain state of vibration, which can be conveyed to others, arousing in them a similar vibration. You see that in everyday actions. I am talking to you. What am I trying to do? I am, so to say, bringing my mind to a certain state of vibration, and the more I succeed in bringing it to that state, the more you will be affected by what I say. All of you know that the day I am more enthusiastic the more you enjoy the lecture. (Vivekananda)

220. *Q*: Some of these facts about human nature shock us out of our idealism, which the mystics would no doubt call false idealism. How can these facts be turned into healing?

A: Truth is always present; it only needs to lift the iron lids of the mind's eye to read its oracles. (Emerson)

221. *Q*: Please review the main lessons governing right relations with both others and ourselves.

A: The highest purpose of intellectual cultivation is to give man a perfect knowledge and command of his own inner self; to render his consciousness its own light. (Novalis)

Outstanding principles to remember

a. Right thinking creates right human relations.
b. You need never be afraid of any other person.
c. Our principal task in life is cosmic self-awakening.

d. Knowledge of these ideas is perfect social security!

e. Use every event, calm or rough, for more self-insight.

f. Observe and learn from your own actions and reactions.

g. Learn to live simply, easily, with self-contentment.

h. All harm to others is automatic self-harm.

i. Let these truths guide your daily experiences.

j Live with these principles about social relations.

4. Let Your Mind Work Wonders for You

222. *Q*: There are so many topics of study, like habits and success and happiness, so how can we avoid getting lost in the maze of all these subjects?

A: At bottom there is but one subject of study . . . the mind. All other subjects may be reduced to that; all other studies bring us back to this study. (Amiel)

223. *Q*: For a long time I was quite sure I possessed a clear mind and wise judgment, so what a shock to see my mistake! But now that I have gone through the humiliation, I find a great sense of relief as well as a new kind of understanding.

A: But now you are awake; it is but a dream you had! For horror's prey in darkness of the night is but our reason's sport in morning light. (Corneille)

224. *Q*: It is a problem to determine which of the modern teachers of these ancient wisdoms are best qualified to help us. Which ones deserve our attention and our respect?

A: Nothing is at last sacred but the integrity of your own mind. (Emerson)

225. *Q*: Both Epictetus and Marcus Aurelius teach that a change of opinion towards a circumstance changes that circumstance as far as the individual is concerned. Could you please explain that principle in another way?

A: There is nothing either good or bad, but thinking makes it so. (Shakespeare)

226. *Q*: Then the correct way to banish harmful conditions

is to banish the belief in harm from our thinking?

A: I saw that all things which occasioned me any anxiety or fear had in themselves nothing of good or evil, except in so far as the mind was moved by them. (Spinoza)

227.   *Q*: In simple language, what is the matter with man?

A: Finally, the mind of man is so constructed that it is taken far more with disguises than with realities. (Erasmus)

228.   *Q*: In what way does a man think illogically?

A: One believes what one wishes to believe. (France)

229.   *Q*: I am very pleased at how my new insight into human nature has swept away many harmful beliefs.

A: It is very necessary that a man should be appraised early in life that it is a masquerade in which he finds himself, for otherwise, there are many things which he will fail to understand. (Schopenhauer)

230.   *Q*: For one thing, I have observed that weakness in people invites tyranny from other weak people who pretend to be strong.

A: Whatever cannot obey itself, is commanded. Such is the nature of living things. (Nietzsche)

231.   *Q*: Is it necessary to retire from the world in order to achieve our inner objectives?

A: Character is constructed in the midst of the tempests of the world. (Goethe)

Great minds are like eagles

232.   *Q*: How does the absorption of lofty principles change and refine our physical habits?

A: Gentleness in the gait is what simplicity is in the dress. Violent gestures or quick movements inspire involuntary disrespect. (Balzac)

233. *Q*: The mystics teach that self-awareness can turn us into real people. I would be helped by having an example of non-aware behaviour.

A: We often inconvenience others, when we fancy we can never possibly do so. (La Rochefoucauld)

234. *Q*: What makes a man whatever he is?

A: As he thinketh in his heart, so is he. (Old Testament)

235. *Q*: I want to show a friend that mystical principles consist of the highest form of common sense, which keeps one out of trouble. Please supply a suitable thought for this.

A: What man in his senses abandons that which is good, to keep company with evil? (Clement)

236. *Q*: Why do human beings generally fail to receive the higher truths which could save them from themselves?

A: They are, in effect, deaf to that internal voice which, nevertheless, calls to them so loud and emphatically. A mere machine is evidently incapable of thinking . . . whereas in man there exists something perpetually prone to expand, and to burst the chains by which it is confined. (Rousseau)

237. *Q*: I sense the existence of a higher intelligence, but there seems to be a wall between us. How can I attain natural oneness with this greater force?

A: Every instrument and tool, if it does that for which it has been made, is well, and yet he who made it is not there. But in things which are put together by nature, there abides in them the power which made them, therefore, the more correct it is to reverence this power. Think that if you live and act according to its will, everything in you is in harmony with intelligence. (Aurelius)

238. *Q*: Sometimes I feel that my understanding has bumped into a fence.

A: God has placed no limit to intellect. (Bacon)

239. *Q*: There must be a reason for it, but I do not understand why the true teachers emphasize cosmic love, instead of offering specific advice about harmony in the family and in friendships.

A: Right is more beautiful than private affection; and love is compatible with universal wisdom. (Emerson)

240. *Q*: In other words, these teachers think from a higher level?

A: Great minds are like eagles, and build their nest in some lofty solitude. (Schopenhauer)

241. *Q*: My difficulty is self-doubt. One minute I think I know how to improve my life, but the next minute I am overwhelmed by uncertainty.

A: Our doubts are traitors, and make us lose the good we oft might win by fearing to attempt. (Shakespeare)

How to be a self-aware individual

242. *Q*: A main mental problem is our absence from ourselves, our inability to be conscious of what we are doing at the time we are doing it. What short phrase can we use for keeping us at home to ourselves?

A: Remember yourself. (Gurdjieff)

243. *Q*: Can you provide an example of how a free and spontaneous mind rolls forward?

A: Perfect kindness acts without thinking of kindness. (Lao-tse)

244. *Q*: I have often wondered why certain people can be very skilled and clever in their business or in artistic work, yet in matters calling for the simplest of good judgment they do the most stupid thing possible.

A: Cleverness is not wisdom. (Euripides)

245. *Q*: There are so few who really know!

A: Excellent things are rare. (Plato)

246. *Q*: Does such old-fashioned technique as making a daily determination to succeed have a place in mystical programmes?

A: The greatest man is he who chooses right with the most invincible resolution. (Seneca)

247. *Q*: I accept the existence of this new way of thinking towards life, and I believe that certain men, like Christ and Buddha, found it. However, it is only a vague concept in my mind. Can you explain my difficulty to me?

A: No man can see *over his own height*. Let me explain what I mean. You cannot see in another man any more than you have in yourself. Your own level strictly determines the extent to which he comes within your understanding. If your intelligence is unawakened, mental qualities in another, even though they be of the highest kind, will have no effect on you at all . . . his higher mental qualities will no more exist for you than colours exist for those who cannot see. (Schopenhauer)

248. *Q*: So if we raise our own level of consciousness, we will also know what the great teachers knew?

A: A principle installed into a good mind brings forth fruit. (Pascal)

249. *Q*: I often feel that we are required to do more than our understanding allows us to do.

A: God is able to do more than man can understand. (Kempis)

250. *Q*: What mental fault prevents happiness?

A: We are no longer happy so soon as we wish to be happier. (Landor)

251. *Q*: Will you please repeat that in another way?

A: Happiness in this world, when it comes, comes incidentally. Make it the object of pursuit, and it leads us a wild-goose chase, and is never attained. (Hawthorne)

An important fact about self-curing

252. *Q*: What is the cure for mental suffering?

A: It follows absolutely, that one who uses his understanding correctly, can fall a prey to no sorrow. (Spinoza)

253. *Q*: How is fear banished?

A: Fear must be entirely banished. The purified soul will fear nothing. (Plotinus)

254. *Q*: Recently I read a lecture by one of those rare men who really knows what he is talking about in spiritual matters. One part of me was afraid to accept the strong truths he offered, but another part was immensely attracted to him. Please comment on this.

A: When a natural discourse paints a passion or an effect, one feels within oneself the truth of what one reads. This feeling was there before, although one did not know it. Therefore, one is inclined to love him who makes us feel it, for he has not shown us his own riches, but ours. (Pascal)

255. *Q*: I can't deny that much of my thinking is mechanical, rather than fresh and spontaneous. I always find myself thinking and saying the same things. I would like to change it, but am not sure as to the method.

A: The wish to be cured is part of the cure. (Seneca)

256. *Q*: Why do most of us change our minds so often and so quickly?

A: Our moods do not believe in each other. (Emerson)

257. *Q*: A friend of mine enjoys these studies, but cannot understand how all this thinking can help her daily actions. What can I tell her?

A: Philosophy is the art of living. (Plutarch)

258. *Q*: It is now clear to me that I have been living mostly from borrowed ideas, so I wish to start all over again and think for myself. This is possible, isn't it?

A: A man of intellect is like an artist who gives a concert without help from anyone else, playing on a single instrument — perhaps a piano, which is a small orchestra in itself. Such a man is a small world in himself, and the effects produced by various instruments together, he produces all by himself, in the unity of his own consciousness. (Schopenhauer)

259. *Q*: Will you please comment on this from the viewpoint of what is usually called mental maturity?

A: When I was a child, I spake as a child, I understood as a child, I thought as a child, but when I became a man, I put away childish things. (New Testament)

260. *Q*: I suppose we must give up our toys, but won't we miss them, won't we feel empty?

A: When the moon shone we did not see the candle. (Shakespeare)

261. *Q*: I was once advised to unlearn many of my acquired ideas which swelled me up with pride. How would you confirm the necessity for this?

A: Humility, like darkness, reveals the heavenly lights. (Thoreau)

262. *Q*: Does this revelation tell us what we need to know about ourselves?

A: Man's true nature, his true good, true virtue, and true religion, are things of which the knowledge is inseparable. (Pascal)

Let self-transformation start right now!

263. Q: Please supply a good general attitude I should maintain throughout my day.

   A: Be free, gay, simple, a child. But be a sturdy child who fears nothing. (Fénelon)

264. Q: I used to think I could find myself by chasing madly around from one exciting event to another, but thanks to these studies I realize that a thousand zeros still add up to zero.

   A: There comes a time when, on the one hand, a vague awakening consciousness stirs the soul, the consciousness of the higher law ... and the sufferings a man endures from the contradictions of life, compel him to renounce the social order and to adopt the new ... And this time has now arrived. (Tolstoy)

265. Q: I have a very active mind, but it does not produce the valuable results I would like.

   A: To be possessed of an energetic mind is not enough; the first requirement is to use it correctly. (Descartes)

266. Q: There is something I do not understand. We have been told that the human mind is a powerful and marvellous instrument, yet we see nothing but chaos and heartbreak all around us. What is the answer to this apparent contradiction?

   A: It is the abuse of our faculties which make us wicked and miserable. Our cares, our anxieties, our griefs, are all owing to ourselves ... If we could be contented with being what we are, we should have no inducement to lament our fate; but we inflict on ourselves a thousand real evils in seeking after an imaginary happiness. (Rousseau)

267. Q: What new value can an individual expect from achieving mental control?

   A: Without effort, he rules all things by the power of his mind. (Xenophanes)

268. *Q*: What could I say to a person who wishes to understand why he behaves as he does?

A: Thought is parent of the deed. (Carlyle)

269. *Q*: We need to be reminded that mental elevation is a supremely important task in life. Please supply such a reminder.

A: Let a prince be guarded with soldiers, attended by counsellors, and protected by a fort, yet if his thoughts disturb him, he is miserable. (Plutarch)

270. *Q*: To meditate upon these self-enriching ideas requires that we free our minds of noises and distractions, but everything around us screams for our attention.

A: The Wise One instills the truth in whoever comes to him yearning for freedom, who follows the true path, calming the tumult of his mind and bringing restfulness. (Shankara)

271. *Q*: Am I correct in thinking that these guiding principles will eventually become a basic part of our nature, so that all guidance is really self-guidance?

A: When we meet with the self thus purified . . . even while here below, we have attained the heights, and need no further guidance. (Plotinus)

Secrets about the laws of the mind

272. *Q*: Intuition has been defined as a higher form of understanding. In what way does it perceive things?

A Intuition is the clear conception of the whole at once. (Lavater)

273. *Q*: If a person learns to listen to this inner voice, will it tell him everything he needs to know?

A: He need not go away from home for instruction. (Terence)

274. *Q*: No matter the direction in which I turn my mind, I feel like a soldier who jumps into a trench for safety, only to find himself facing enemy rifles.

A: To win true peace, a man needs to feel himself directed, pardoned, and sustained by a supreme power, to feel himself on the right road, at the point where God would have him be — in harmony with God and the universe. This reliance gives strength and calm. (Amiel)

275. *Q*: Are there definite laws of the mind whose understanding will help us?

A: All things obey fixed laws. (Lucretius)

276. *Q*: Please describe one such law.

A: Great men are they who see that spiritual is stronger than any material force, that thoughts rule the world. (Emerson)

277. *Q*: May we have an example of how this law operates within us, perhaps to increase our skill in whatever we do?

A: The more we do, the more we can do; the more busy we are, the more leisure we have. (Hazlitt)

278. *Q*: My work as a doctor uncovers the bad mental diets of many people, I mean, they feed upon negativities, like bitterness and argument. What is the esoteric explanation of this?

A: A man that has no virtue in himself, ever envies virtue in others, for men's minds will either feed upon their own good or upon others' evil, and who lacks the one will prey upon the other. (Bacon)

279. *Q*: Is it possible to make alert efforts without straining ourselves?

A: The thoughts that come often unsought, and, as it were, drop into the mind, are commonly the most valuable of any we have. (Locke)

280. *Q:* How would we feel the influence of a truly superior mind?

A: The great make us feel, first of all, the indifference of circumstances. They call into activity the higher perceptions, and subdue the low habits of comfort and luxury; but the higher perceptions find their objects everywhere; only the low habits need palaces and banquets. (Emerson)

281. *Q:* What is the difference between a fully enlightened mind and a mind still struggling towards the heights?

A: Little minds are too much hurt by little events. Great minds understand all of them, and remain untouched. (La Rochefoucauld)

You can live your own life

282. *Q:* I need assistance in abolishing certain habits of behaviour which usually lead to trouble. Can right thinking solve this problem?

A: Thought is the key to all treasure. (Balzac)

283. *Q:* I want to live my own life, but people think you are cold and selfish unless you join their silly activities. I suspect this may be false guilt on my part.

A: I would rather sit on a pumpkin, and have it all to myself, than to be crowded on a velvet cushion. (Thoreau)

284. *Q:* What is the connection between self-knowledge and self-discontent?

A: Those who do not observe the movements of their own minds must of necessity be unhappy. (Aurelius)

285. *Q:* What benefit comes to us as we carry these principles into our daily life in business and at home?

A: The chief result gained by experience is *clearness of view.* This is what distinguishes the man of mature age . . . it is only then that he sees things plainly, and takes them for what they really are, while in earlier years he saw a

phantom-world, put together with the whims and imaginations of his own mind . . . the real world was hidden from
him, or the vision of it distorted. The first thing that
experience does is to free us from the phantoms of the
mind. (Schopenhauer)

286. *Q*: I want to think for myself, to not accept a position
as right just because the masses insist it is right.

   A: A hundred thousand sheep are not more instructive
than one sheep. (Amiel)

287. *Q*: Is there a point along the spiritual path when we
become aware of new values and new directions, I mean, will
we see a clear difference in the way we think and feel and
act?

   A: There is a moment . . . at which flattery and
falsehood can no longer deceive, and innocence itself can no
longer be misled. (Junius)

288. *Q*: What thought can begin to shake us loose from the
illusion that others have power over us?

   A: Most powerful is he who has himself in his
power. (Seneca)

289. *Q*: I have been thinking of all the reasons why we must
work diligently to turn the light of consciousness upon
ourselves. One of the best reasons is that it leads us out of the
pain of envy and competition with our neighbours. What
reason can you add?

   A: Just as a candle cannot burn without fire, men
cannot live without a spiritual life. (Buddha)

290. *Q*: In a crisis I am sometimes overcome by impulsive
reactions which only make things worse. Where does correction begin?

   A: The improvement of the mind improves the heart
and corrects the understanding. (Agathon)

291. *Q*: Please comment on the connection between

common sense and these higher revelations of truth.

A: It is not necessary to think of revelation as a source of knowledge which is either contrary to reason or above reason . . . On the contrary, it would not be difficult to show that the true idea of revelation, that which is most honouring to God, is at the same time that which is most ennobling to man — the idea, that is, of a revelation which addresses itself, not to the ear or the logical understanding only, but to the whole spiritual nature. (Caird)

How to expand your mental powers

292. *Q*: What basic idea can we reflect upon during the day, in order to expand our awareness of things as they really are?

A: Self-reverence, self-knowledge, self-control, these three alone lead life to sovereign power. (Tennyson)

293. *Q*: People tell me they wish power to clear their lives of nagging problems, but say they do not know where to start.

A: There is a great deal of umapped country within us which would have to be taken into account in explanation of our gusts and storms. (Eliot)

294. *Q*: Please start us towards exploring this country.

A: The first lesson, then, is to sit for some time and let the mind run on. The mind is bubbling up all the time. It is like that monkey jumping about. Let the monkey jump as much as he can; you simply watch and wait. Knowledge is power says the proverb, and that is true. Until you know what the mind is doing you cannot control it. Give it the full length of the reins; many most hideous thoughts may come into it; you will be astonished that it was possible for you to think such thoughts. But you will find that each day the mind's vagaries are becoming less and less violent, that each day it is becoming calmer . . . until at last it will be under perfect control, but we must patiently practise every day. (Vivekananda)

295. *Q:* You said that when there is something right in us, we are attracted to the rightness of these higher cosmic truths. I have a long way to go, but already I marvel at the new world I have entered.

A: It was through the feeling of wonder that men now and at first began to philosophize. (Aristotle)

296. *Q:* How can we prevent the loss of helpful insights we have acquired?

A: A thought once awakened does not slumber. (Carlyle)

297. *Q:* I often feel judged by others, which is a form of mental slavery I would like to abolish.

A: Who in the world, then, is the man who has any authority to make any declaration about you? (Epictetus)

298. *Q:* How do our daily actions connect with these higher truths?

A: To be a philospher is not merely to have subtle thoughts, nor even to found a school, but so to love wisdom as to live, according to its dictates, a life of simplicity, independence, magnanimity, and trust. (Thoreau)

299. *Q:* Please explain how a right mind makes right actions.

A: A capacity for self-recollection — from withdrawal from the outward to the inward — is in fact the condition of all noble and useful activity. (Amiel)

300. *Q:* There seems to be an inner impulse that drives us forward, even against our weary wishes to give up. What is the nature of this encouraging energy?

A: We feel that we are greater than we know. (Wordsworth)

301. *Q:* I never quite know what step to take next.

A: Walk on! (Zen)

Absorb these uplifting thoughts

a. Release your mental powers by learning all about them.
b. Whatever we are is determined by whatever we think.
c. There is no limit to your mental expansion.
d. Practise daily at being a self-aware individual.
e. You can use your own mind for all self-curing.
f. Starting today, let your mind transform your life.
g. Your deeper mind knows all the needed answers to life!
h. Learn to think easily, casually, naturally.
i. Right thinking frees you of a false sense of guilt.
j. Awakened mental powers can never be lost.

5. The Way to Lasting Peace and Happiness

302. Q: Please describe the nature of a truly victorious life.

A: A happy life consists in a mind which is free, upright, undaunted and steadfast, beyond the influence of fear or desire. (Seneca)

303. Q: What is the highest happiness of man?

A: What greater pleasure is there than to find myself the one thing that I ought to be, and the whole thing that I ought to be? (Suso)

304. Q: I am caught in a mental contradiction, but at least am aware of it. One part of my mind insists that others are responsible for my troubles, while another part tells me to stop blaming others and to see myself as my only problem. What fact can strengthen the right voice?

A: No man is damaged by an action which is not his own. (Epictetus)

305. Q: It is strange, but I often feel guilty about enjoying myself, and I have noticed the same feeling in others. I believe it is a false feeling, but what part should enjoyment play in life?

A: The highest enjoyment is that of being contented with ourselves. It is in order to deserve this contentment that we are placed here on earth and endowed with liberty. (Rousseau)

306. Q: But what can a person do when all his familiar and established plans for happiness break down and fail him?

A: Let him lovingly cast all his thoughts and cares, and his sins, too, as it were, on that unknown Will. Beyond this unknown will of God, he must desire and purpose nothing; neither way, nor rest, nor work, neither this nor that, nor wholly subject and offer himself up to this unknown will. (Tauler)

307. *Q*: Many people pretend to be happy, but are unaware that they are merely playing a role. What is the difference between artificial happiness and true happiness?

A: False happiness renders men stern and proud, and that happiness is never communicated. True happiness renders them kind and sensible, and that happiness is always shared. (Montesquieu)

308. *Q*: It seems that we must have a fondness for what is right.

A: For a happy life is joy in the truth. (Augustine)

309. *Q*: The open or subtle competition between men for power and prestige is an obvious factor in turning life sour. What do men who live in reality say about such competition?

A: If two angels were sent down from heaven — one to conduct an empire, and the other to sweep a street — they would feel no inclination to change employments. (Newton)

How happiness comes by itself

310. *Q*: What mental technique might we put into operation for abolishing unhappiness?

A: It is most important for anyone who is capable of higher and nobler thoughts to keep his mind from being so completely engrossed with private affairs and ungracious troubles as to let them take up all his attention and crowd out worthier matters, for that is, in a very real sense, to lose sight of the true end of life. (Schopenhauer)

311. *Q*: I can testify as to the rightness of these studies, for I know full well how they describe my own condition! For

one thing, I am beginning to see the uselessness of wishing to have what others possess.

A: Before we passionately desire anything which another enjoys, we should examine into the happiness of its possessor. (La Rochefoucauld)

312. *Q*: I have difficulty understanding the basic cause of mental and emotional suffering. Will you please explain it as simply as possible?

A: We do not content ourselves with the life we have in ourselves and in our own being; we desire to live an imaginary life in the mind of others, and for this purpose we desire to shine. We labour unceasingly to adorn and preserve this imaginary existence, and neglect the real. And if we possess calmness or generosity or truthfulness, we are eager to make it known, so as to attach these virtues to that imaginary existence. (Pascal)

313. *Q*: So the basic cure is to get at the basic cause. In other words, happiness comes by itself when we cease to live in illusions about ourselves?

A: When the imaginary self melts away. (Shankara)

314. *Q*: Is it truly possible to change what happens to us in daily experiences, I mean, change for the better?

A: If we will lift up the mind. (Boehme)

315. *Q*: Would you say that growth towards peace consists in making right choices, like choosing to understand our minds instead of choosing to dislike ourselves?

A: Each man in his perception of truth is like a traveller who walks by aid of a lantern whose light is cast before him: he does not see what as yet has not been revealed by the beams, he does not see the path he has left behind . . . but at any given step he sees that which the lantern reveals, and he is always at liberty to choose one side of the road or the other. (Tolstoy)

316. *Q*: To feel good we must obviously choose what is truly right for us, but that is our problem. We are so confused regarding what is truly right.

A: That is always best which gives me to myself. The sublime is excited in me by the great stoical doctrine, Obey thyself. That which shows God in me, fortifies me. (Emerson)

317. *Q*: By what method can I help my spouse get over nervous irritability which keeps our home in an uproar?

A: All things must be set right in yourself first, before you can rightly assist others towards the attaining to the same state. (Law)

How mystic truths work for you

318. *Q*: Please supply a rule for starting out towards inner newness.

A: The first was never to accept anything for true which I did not clearly know to be such. (Descartes)

319. *Q*: Life gives us so many things to do, it is wise to place first things first. What is the correct order of procedure for life in general?

A: Seek ye first the kingdom of God, and his righteousness, and all these things shall be added unto you. (Jesus)

320. *Q*: We seem to be on a futile march. Our desired happiness recedes before our eyes as we approach it.

A: Let each one examine his thoughts, and he will find them all occupied with the past and the future. We scarcely ever think of the present, and if we think of it, it is only to take light from it to arrange the future . . . So we never live, but we hope to live; and, as we are always preparing to be happy, it is inevitable we should never be so. (Pascal)

321. *Q*: What is the correction?

A: Confine yourself to the present. (Aurelius)

322.   *Q*: I was recently upset when my plans for moving to a new home were blocked by unexpected circumstances. According to esoteric doctrines, could I have maintained perfect poise in spite of everything?

A: The mind is the master over every kind of fortune; it acts in both ways, being the cause of its own happiness and its own misery. (Seneca)

323.   *Q*: Then sadness is merely a wrong state of mind?

A: All gloom is but a dream and a shadow . . . cheerfulness is the real truth. (Hawthorne)

324.   *Q*: I am trying to understand more clearly that self-contentment is the only contentment. Will you shed more light on this?

A: When I see an anxious man, I say, 'What does this man want?' If he did not want something which is not in his power, how could he be anxious? For this reason, a lute player when he is singing by himself has no anxiety, but when he goes to the theatre, he is anxious, even if he has a good voice and plays well on the lute, for he not only wishes to sing well, but also to obtain applause, which is not in his power. (Epictetus)

325.   *Q*: How do these mystical truths work on us, I mean, how do they change us, what do we become?

A: Man is only what he becomes – profound truth, but he becomes only what he is – truth still more profound. (Amiel)

326.   *Q*: Why do so many people fail to discover these profound details about their own deliverance?

A: Errors, like straws, upon the surface flow; he who would search for pearls must dive below. (Dryden)

327.   *Q*: I would be happier if I could see myself taking long leaps out of the spiritual desert into the meadows.

A: A true-devoted pilgrim is not weary to measure kingdoms with his feeble steps. (Shakespeare)

No secrets of life are hidden from you

328. *Q*: What prevents us from finding lasting contentment?

A: There comes for ever something between us and what we deem our happiness. (Byron)

329. *Q*: What sort of things?

A: We are the creatures of imagination, passion and self-will, more than of reason, or even of self-interest ... Even in the common transactions and daily intercourse of life, we are governed by whim, caprice, prejudice or accident. The falling of a teacup puts us out of temper for the day. (Hazlitt)

330. *Q*: I understand how we must be the architect of our own happiness, but fate constantly thwarts our intentions.

A: Happiness lies in the consciousness we have of it, and by no means in the way the future keeps its promises. (Sand)

331. *Q*: If we could only find a way to make this fact a guiding light in everything that happens to us.

A: Courage comes next to prudence as a quality of mind very essential to happiness ... Our motto should be *'No Surrender'*, and far from yielding to the ills of life, let us take fresh courage from misfortune ... Let our attitude be such that we would not quake even if the world fell in ruins about us. (Schopenhauer)

332. *Q*: I am newly inspired by my introduction to esotericism, but must we not guard against substituting the inspirational for the practical?

A: The useful and the beautiful are never separated. (Periander)

333.   *Q*: What cosmic law governs our level of happiness?

A: Whilst a man seeks good ends, he is strong by the whole strength of nature . . . The perception of this law of laws awakens in the mind a sentiment which we call the religious sentiment, and which makes our highest happiness. Wonderful is its power to charm and to command. It is a mountain air. (Emerson)

334.   *Q*: What is the esoteric definition of happiness?

A: A happy life is one which is in accordance with its own nature. (Seneca)

335.   *Q*: If nature is good, why do we suffer from evil?

A: There exists no other evil in nature than what you either do or suffer, and you are equally the author of both . . . Particular evil exists only in the sentiment of the suffering being; and this sentiment is not given to man by nature, but is of his own acquisition . . . Take away our errors and our vices . . . take away, in short, everything that is the work of man, and all that remains is good. (Rousseau)

336.   *Q*: The mystics say that nothing is hidden from the man who really wants to find out. How is this accomplished?

A: I plunge into myself and all things know. (Sufism)

337.   *Q*: Is it correct to say that the more we have of our true self, the less we need other things?

A: Few things are needed to make a wise man happy; nothing can make a foolish man content, and that is why most men are miserable. (La Rochefoucauld)

How to banish painful imagination

338.   *Q*: You state quite correctly that our minds often refuse to see our actual unhappiness, because we prefer to live in dreamland. How can we conquer this self-evasion? Are our emotions more honest than our minds?

A: We are not miserable without feeling it. (Pascal)

339. *Q*: It is a new but sensible thought to me that the first step towards personal peace is to calmly be aware of our lack of peace.

A: The beginning of philosophy to him at least who enters on it in the right way and by the door, is a consciousness of his own weakness and inability about necessary things. (Epictetus)

340. *Q*: I know that esoteric teachings stress the need for faithful self-examination, but what is its purpose?

A: If by patience, if by watching, I can secure one new ray of light, can feel myself elevated . . . shall I not watch ever? (Thoreau)

341. *Q*: I practise honest self-examination, but am sometimes shocked at what I see in myself.

A: Truth above all, even when it upsets and overwhelms us! (Amiel)

342. *Q*: And this begins an entirely new kind of happiness?

A: There is no greater delight than to be conscious of sincerity in self-examination. (Mencius)

343. *Q*: I don't understand why philosophers and religious teachers spend so much time talking about human sorrow. Most people appear reasonably happy.

A: What private griefs they have, alas! (Shakespeare)

344. *Q*: My imagination is constantly running off unhappy scenes from my past. I don't like the strange hold these scenes have on me.

A: This pulling out of the imagination which I am recommending, will also forbid us to summon up the memory of past misfortune, to paint a dark picture of the injustice or harm that has been done us, the losses we have sustained, the insults, slights and annoyances to which we have been exposed, for to do that is to arouse fresh life into all those hateful passions long laid asleep — the anger and resentment which disturb and pollute our nature. (Schopenhauer)

345. *Q*: What will help us to work on ourselves with greater sincerity?

A: Let us not forget that man can never get away from himself. (Goethe)

346. *Q*: Esotericism cautions us against getting carried away by excited emotions which masquerade as feelings of joy. Will you please provide an example of legitimate emotions?

A: When we are unhurried and wise, we perceive that only great and worthy things have any permanent and absolute existence, that petty fears and petty pleasures are but the shadow of reality. This is always exhilarating and sublime. (Thoreau)

347. *Q*: My observations of other people reveal how much they suffer from feeling unnoticed and unappreciated. What is the answer to this?

A: The silence that accepts merit as the most natural thing in the world, is the highest applause. (Emerson)

The interior man is always free!

348. *Q*: The mystics teach that man is already complete, needing nothing to be happy, but man *is* unhappy.

A: The heart is like a musical instrument of many strings, in which all the chords need to be played in harmony. (Saadi)

349. *Q*: Why are people who have succeeded in various ways just as unhappy as they were before winning success?

A: If we cannot find contentment in ourselves, it is useless to seek it elsewhere. (La Rochefoucauld)

350. *Q*: The way you have simplified these truths has been of great benefit. My question is, how can we win more of

these perfect moments when we are free of our cares and confusions, that is, when we are detached from ourselves?

A: All that tends to purify and elevate the mind will assist you in this attainment, and facilitate the approach and recurrence of these happy intervals. (Plotinus)

351. *Q*: What is the answer to those who feel that life in general has treated them unfairly?

A: Nature never deceives us; it is always we who deceive ourselves. (Rousseau)

352. *Q*: I cannot reconcile the fact of a riotous world with the fact of inner peace.

A: The exterior man may be undergoing trials, but the interior man is quite free. (Eckhart)

353. *Q*: But the pressures and the demands of the outer world are so insistent.

A: It is in your power to be free from all compulsions, and to remain in the greatest tranquillity of mind, even if all the world cries out against you as much as it chooses. (Aurelius)

354. *Q*: All my life I tried to be happy by letting other people tell me what I needed, but now I see how they used my problems to evade their own problems. It is a genuine pleasure to let these studies make everything clear at last, especially regarding the necessity for inner harmony.

A: There is nothing pleasurable except what is in harmony with the utmost depths of our divine nature. (Suso)

355. *Q*: There must be a good reason why the mystics declare we must go beyond the frontier of shallow human reasoning.

A: Our reason is so weak that a trifle is enough to trouble and intoxicate it. (Cherbuliez)

356. *Q*: Since we need to acquire constructive attitudes, please mention one.

A: Give me liberty to know. (Milton)

357. *Q*: I have recently become aware of a mental imp which has nagged me for many years. I am compelled to constantly justify myself before others, which is tiring. Does inner newness bring release?

A: The victor need not explain. (Gracián)

How to recognize an authentic teacher

358. *Q*: What reassurance could I give to a friend whose search for a new life has been unsuccessful up to this point?

A: You traverse the world in search of happiness, which is within the reach of every man; a contented mind confers it on all. (Horace)

359. *Q*: What could I tell this friend to help cancel his belief that exterior success can fulfill him?

A: Towards the throne they all strive: it is their madness — as if happiness sat on the throne. (Nietzsche)

360. *Q*: A group of us at the office have been discussing the topic of individual happiness. Will you please supply an idea which I might add to the discussion?

A: The greatness and the wretchedness of men are so evident that the true religion must necessarily teach us both that there is in man some great source of greatness, and a great source of wretchedness. It must then give us an explanation of these astonishing contradictions. In order to make man happy, it must prove to him that there is a God, and we ought to love him, that our true happiness is to be in him, and our sole evil to be separated from him. (Pascal)

361. *Q*: Where does the idea of prayer enter into our studies? People pray for happiness, but not much seems to happen.

A: Prayer as a means to effect a private end is theft and meanness. It supposes dualism in nature and consciousness. As soon as the man is at one with God he will not beg. He will then see prayer in all action. (Emerson)

362. *Q*: It is clear that frustration arises from not seeing things as they really are. What is an instance of wrong judgment towards other people?

A: Those who are believed to be the most mild and humble are usually the most ambitious and envious. (Spinoza)

363. *Q*: Most of us chase frantically around in our attempts to build security, but those men who know what life is all about have a unique leisureliness. How can they afford to be so casual in a flustered world?

A: Who stands already on heaven's topmost dome needs not to search for ladders. (Rumi)

364. *Q*: If we were to meet a man who sees things as they really are, how could we recognize him as such?

A: It takes a wise man to discover a wise man. (Xenophanes)

365. *Q*: You have helped me to see that a problem cannot be solved on its own level; that self-elevation is the answer to every unhappiness. Will you please repeat this fact in a new way?

A: We can console ourselves for not having great talents as we console ourselves for not having great places. We can be above both in our hearts. (Vauvenargues)

366. *Q*: People usually attribute their unhappiness to superficial causes, like lack of money. Will you supply us with a deep and real reason?

A: The cause of misery is the clash between the different forces of nature, one dragging one way, and another dragging another, rendering permanent happiness impossible. (Vivekananda)

367.   *Q*: What can free us of these inner contradictions?

A: The conscious self is that which remains constant in its pure universality through all particular, changeful experiences . . . it has the capacity to transcend that opposition and to think a higher unity which comprehends. (Caird)

Your glimpse of a new world

368.   *Q*: Please give us a thought about happiness for our careful reflection.

A: To believe that happiness exists in a feverish ambition, rather than in a tender and simple affection, is to believe that the immensity of the sea will more readily quench thirst than the pure, clear water of a humble fountain. (Castelar)

369.   *Q*: These teachings take away many of the activities of which we were fond, but which we now see as useless. What new activities will capture our fondness?

A: That which causes us to think is dear to us, and everything which gives even a small impulse to our faculties is agreeable. (Lavater)

370.   *Q*: What determines whether we go swiftly or slowly along the mystic path?

A: God offers to every mind its choice between truth and repose. (Emerson)

371.   *Q*: The mystic masters have described my mental state much too accurately! Quite frankly, my mind is a museum, incapable of displaying anything fresh and spontaneous. If I understand correctly, this awareness is in itself a long step towards newness.

A: The beginning of philosophy is to know the condition of one's own mind. If a man recognizes its weaknesses, he will not wish to apply it to important questions. (Epictetus)

372. Q: I now know several positive mental states to cultivate, but would like to know of various negative states, so as to avoid them.

A: Some persons depress their own minds, despond at the first difficulty; and conclude that making any progress in knowledge, farther than serves their ordinary business, is above their capacities. (Locke)

373. Q: What determines our fate and destiny?

A: What I will is fate. (Milton)

374. Q: Peace among human beings can come only with the unity of all hearts and minds. What cosmic fact can help us achieve this unity?

A: All are but parts of one stupendous whole. (Pope)

375. Q: A previous point of yours has given me unusual encouragement, so I would like it repeated. You said that only when our world falls apart do we have incentive for finding a new and real world.

A: It is only when everything, even love, fails, that, with a flash, man finds out how vain, how dream-like is this world. Then he catches a glimpse . . . of the beyond. It is only by giving up this world that the other comes; never through holding on to this one. (Vivekananda)

376. Q: Some people seem to have a greater degree of spiritual contentment than others. What determines the difference?

A: There is an esoteric doctrine . . . each man enters into God so much as God enters into him. (Amiel)

377. Q: My awareness of the need for an open mind has changed everything for me!

A: What a light is here for those that can bear or love the light! (Law)

Summary of ideas about happiness

a. Happiness consists in being a real and free person.
b. An agitated imagination prevents happiness.
c. You choose life-enjoyment by choosing cosmic truth!
d. Live only in the reality of the present moment.
e. Never be discouraged in your search for trueness.
f. Study the mystical laws which govern peace of mind.
g. Do not be afraid to face any present distress.
h. Do not mistake passing excitement for lasting peace.
i. Your interior self is always free and contented.
j. Practise these principles with enthusiasm.

6. How to Gain More Strength and Confidence

378. *Q*: What is the secret of the strength of the mystic masters?

A: Great men stand like solitary towers in the city of God, and secret passages, running deep beneath external nature, give their thoughts intercourse with higher intelligences, which strengthens and consoles them, and of which the labourers on the surface do not even dream. (Longfellow)

379. *Q*: If I were to follow the example of men who have achieved steadfast confidence, what would I do?

A: Use the light that is in you to recover your natural clearness of sight. (Lao-tse)

380. *Q*: You say that new power fills us as we blend with cosmic rules. Please explain.

A: Once possessed of the principle, it is equally easy to make forty or forty thousand applications of it. (Emerson)

381. *Q*: It makes no difference what we call this Higher Power — whether God or Truth, Reality or Creator, but all of us have this inner yearning for something superior to our everyday selves. How can we make this lofty contact?

A: You ask, 'How can we know the Infinite?' I answer, not by reason. It is the office of reason to distinguish and define. The Infinite, therefore, cannot be ranked among its objects. You can only apprehend the Infinite by a faculty superior to reason, by entering into a state in which you are your finite self no longer, in which the Divine Essence is communicated to you. This is Ecstasy. It is the liberation of your mind from its finite consciousness. (Plotinus)

382. *Q*: Can you describe the way in which our inner strengths grow as we persist in self-discovery?

A: They may be compared to the commanders of armies, whose forces usually increase in proportion to their victories . . . For he truly engages in battle who endeavours to surmount all the difficulties and errors which prevent him from reaching the knowledge of truth. (Descartes)

383. *Q*: I stand solidly on these principles when all is going smoothly, but sag somewhat when a psychic storm breaks out.

A: Be like the promontory against which the waves continually break, but which stands firm and tames the fury of the water around it. (Aurelius)

384. *Q*: Please suggest a technique for making the mind the master of any task which the hands are required to do.

A: Careful attention to one thing often proves superior to genius. (Cicero)

The power of honest self-facing

385. *Q*: The true teachings, including the New Testament, say that we grow strong by first becoming weak, that wisdom comes by abandoning our usual wisdom. I do not understand this idea of self-growth through self-loss.

A: The more the marble wastes, the more the statue grows. (Michelangelo)

386. *Q*: I understand this to mean we must lose everything false and wrong in us, such as artificial behaviour and imaginary virtues.

A: Our salvation consists wholly in being saved from ourselves. (Law)

387. *Q*: It may be shocking to reveal our weakness to

ourselves, but of course it is necessary. How can we learn about our weak points?

A: Observe yourselves. (Pascal)

388. *Q*: What might we see in ourselves which would finally prove to be valuable self-knowledge?

A: To affect a quality, and to plume yourself upon it, is just to confess that you do not have it. Whether it is courage, or learning, or intellect, or wit, or success with women, or riches, or social position, or whatever else it may be that a man boasts of, you may conclude by his boasting about it that this is precisely the direction in which he is rather weak, for if a man really possesses any faculty to the full, it will not occur to him to make a great show of affecting it; he is quite content to know that he has it. (Schopenhauer)

389. *Q*: No doubt we must become aware of our faults if we are to correct them, but it takes courage to face ourselves, which we often lack.

A: God never makes us sensible of our weaknesses, except to give us of his strength. (Fénelon)

390. *Q*: It is not easy to admit, but I am sometimes easily influenced and persuaded by people who want something from me. Far too often I end up victimized. I don't like this weakness in myself.

A: I have a body on which other bodies act, and which acts reciprocally upon them. This reciprocal action is certain; but my will is independent of my senses. I can either consent to, or resist their impressions. I am either vanquished or victor, and can perceive clearly within myself when I act according to my will, and when I submit to be governed by my passions. I always have the power to will. (Rousseau)

391. *Q*: I have always seen myself as someone who values religion and philosophy, yet I feel cramped by that very self-image. If I am deceiving myself, I want to know about it.

A: Under a pretext of spirituality we are always checking legitimate aspirations. We have lost the mystical sense, and what is religion without mysticism? — a rose without perfume. (Amiel)

392. *Q*: I do not wish to be a part of the complaining attitude which so many people have towards life. What attitude can I adopt to keep myself separate and adventurous?

A: I count life just a stuff to try the soul's strength on. (Browning)

How to gain lasting self-strength

393. *Q*: Will you please explain what the mystics mean by giving up our human identities and human values? What is the purpose, what is the result?

A: When you thus cease to be finite, you become one with the Infinite. In the reduction of your soul to its simplest self, its divine essence, you realize this Union, this Identity. (Plotinus)

394. *Q*: And this new state is one of authentic and permanent self-strength?

A: Speak the truth, and all nature and all spirits help you with unexpected furtherance. (Emerson)

395. *Q*: I need more confidence to face the future.

A: All things change, yet we need not fear anything new. (Aurelius)

396. *Q*: You have said that a first step towards cosmic strength is to dislike our states of weakness. What particular weakness might be a good start?

A: A man's exact imitation of the song of the nightingale displeases us when we discover that it is mimicry, and not the nightingale. (Kant)

397. *Q:* So a man's great technique for becoming a real person is to detect and shun the false?

A: He has chosen the highway; he will advance. *(Bhagavad-Gita)*

398. *Q:* What is the connection between inner strength and periods of solitude? It seems we must sometimes stand apart from others to prevent drainage of our energies.

A: Petrarch gives a similar reason for wishing to be alone — that tender spirit, so strong and constant in his love of seclusion! The streams, the plains and woods know well, he says, how he has tried to escape the perverse and stupid people who have missd the way to heaven. (Schopenhauer)

399. *Q:* I believe it is correct to say that love has a unique power of its own.

A: Love sees what no eye sees; love hears what no ear hears. (Lavater)

400. *Q:* How can we conquer the weakness of getting so easily displeased by other people?

A: If we were faultless, we should not be so much annoyed by the defects of those with whom we associate. If we were to acknowledge honestly that we have not virtue enough to bear patiently with our neighbour's weaknesses, we should show our own imperfection, and this alarms our vanity. (Fénelon)

401. *Q:* I have noticed that many people do not know what is meant by inner strength. Some think that outbursts of emotion indicate personal power. What do you say about this?

A: In the same degree in which a man's mind is nearer to freedom from all passion, in the same degree also is it nearer to strength. (Aurelius)

Why you should associate with these truths

402. *Q*: I have had an interesting inner experience during the last few months. With increasing force, nothing seems important except the gathering of esoteric information.

A: The more we know, the greater our thirst for knowledge. The water-lily, in the midst of waters, opens its leaves and expands its petals at the first pattering of showers, and rejoices in the raindrops with a quicker sympathy than the parched shrub in the sandy desert. (Coleridge)

403. *Q*: If a person wants assistance, he must find it somewhere, but how can he know he has found the right harbour of help?

A: He need go nowhere, because wherever he is, that which is to save him, and that which he is to be saved from, is always with him. (Law)

404. *Q*: Is freedom our natural and original state?

A: I am as free as Nature first made man, ere the base laws of servitude began. (Dryden)

405. *Q*: What happens when we realize our actual liberty?

A: Then flows into us knowledge — an inner revelation which preserves our spirit open, and, lifting us above all images and all disturbance, brings us to an inward silence. Here the divine inspiration is a secret whispering in the inner ear. (Ruysbroeck)

406. *Q*: How can a person speed up the process of inner harmony?

A: His aim should be to concentrate and simplify, and so to expand his being . . . and so to float upwards towards the divine fountain of being whose stream flows within him. (Plotinus)

407. *Q*: I dread that my fortune may be bad.

A: Fortune dreads the brave. (Seneca)

408.   Q: I can see the gold in merely associating with these higher facts.

A: A man who desires to excel should work with those things that are in themselves most excellent. (Epictetus)

409.   Q: Please give us something to think about regarding strength and confidence.

A: Without courage, there cannot be truth, and without truth there can be no other virtue. (Scott)

410.   Q: History proves over and over again that the masses never follow a teacher of genuine strength, at least not for long. Is this because, as the teachers themselves point out, darkness dislikes the light?

A: Mental superiority of any kind always tends to isolate its possessor; people run away from him out of pure hatred, and say all manner of bad things about him by way of justifying their actions. (Schopenhauer)

411.   Q: But suppose a man reverses his attitude, I mean, he now prefers to come home to himself, instead of wandering the psychic jungles. I imagine he will now see the strength of a teacher in a new light.

A: When we see those whom it inhabits, we are appraised of new degrees of greatness. From that inspiration the man comes back with a changed tone. (Emerson)

Be the captain of your own psychic ship!

412.   Q: You say that strength must always be solitary, that we cannot gain it from a crowd, but isn't it a sign of power when an organized group marches in unison towards one direction?

A: The majority of men are, as it were, suspended in the air, like toy balloons; every breath of wind moves them. (Nietzsche)

413.   Q: Then we cannot trust the wisdom of aggressive crowds?

A: Loud clamour is always more or less insane. (Carlyle)

414. *Q*: It is obvious that some teachers dwell in total freedom from earthly burdens. May we know the basic process by which they arrived?

A: This is when the inmost of the spirit is sunk and dissolved in the inmost of the Divine Nature, and thus new-made and transformed. (Tauler)

415. *Q*: How can we prevent the loss of strength and energy?

A: Our life is frittered away by detail . . . Simplify, simplify. (Thoreau)

416. *Q*: Only recently have I become aware of the tremendous value of self-responsibility, which has awakened new energies. How does esotericism teach this virtue?

A: Physician, heal thyself. (Jesus)

417. *Q*: I feel that my past failures may have disqualified me for changing my fortunes today.

A: What you do still betters what is done. (Shakespeare)

418. *Q*: I feel powerless in the face of my own weaknesses. It would help to have a plan for making me the captain of my own psychic ship.

A: Erase your imaginations by often saying to yourself, 'Now it is in my power to let no badness be in this spirit, no craving nor any disturbance at all, but looking at all things I see what is their nature, and I use each according to its value.' Remember this power which you have from nature. (Aurelius)

419. *Q*: From the mystical viewpoint, what is genius?

A: The first and last thing which is required of genius is the love of truth. (Goethe)

420. *Q*: Is the opportunity for finding fresh strength always available?

A: It is always with us, but there must be an opening of the heart to it, and though it is always there, yet it is only felt and found by those who are attentive to it, depend upon, and humbly wait for it. (Law)

421. *Q*: I would never have believed it a few months ago, but now I see how we carelessly permit other people to drain us of energy.

A: Make not a close friend of a melancholy, sad person. He will be sure to increase your adversity and decrease your good fortune. He goes always heavily loaded, and you must bear half. (Fénelon)

422. *Q*: How can we allow our emotions to contribute to our growing strength?

A: Through zeal, knowledge is gained, through lack of zeal, knowledge is lost. Let a man who knows this double path of gain and loss, thus place himself that knowledge may grow. (Buddha)

How to spend your energy profitably

423. *Q*: What is an example of self-defeating effort?

A: The effort people make as far as possible to conceal their misfortunes, and to put the best face they can upon them, for fear lest their misfortunes may show how much they are to blame. (Schopenhauer)

424. *Q*: I need more self-strength in general. What can I rely upon to build it?

A: Relying on what? Not on reputation nor on wealth nor on the power of the law, but on his own strength . . . for these are the only things which make men free. (Epictetus)

425. *Q*: It is only a small stream of insight at the present time, but I do see the absolute necessary for building my life upon spiritual and psychological foundations.

A: To see small beginnings is clearness of sight. (Lao-tse)

426. *Q*: Please define spiritual courage.

A: True fortitude I take to be quiet possession of a man's self, and an undisturbed doing his duty, whatever evil besets or danger lies in his way. (Locke)

427. *Q*: How can we overcome doubt in ourselves?

A: Ever building, building to the clouds, still building higher, and never reflecting that the poor narrow basis cannot sustain the giddy tottering column. (Schiller)

428. *Q*: What do we need to know about spiritual heroism?

A: Heroism is the brilliant triumph of the soul over the flesh, that is to say, over fear, fear of poverty, of suffering . . . There is no serious piety without heroism. Heroism is the dazzling and glorious concentration of courage. (Amiel)

429. *Q*: The courage to stand alone?

A: Heroism works in contradiction to the voice of mankind, and in contradiction, for a time, to the voice of the great and good. Heroism is an obedience to a secret impulse of an individual's character. (Emerson)

430. *Q*: By what method does a mystic master keep himself in strong and spontaneous activity?

A: The sage attends to the inner, and not to the outer. (Lao-tse)

431. *Q*: And this provides a permanent contentment?

A: To be strong is to be happy. (Longfellow)

432. *Q*: I am aware of how much valuable energy we waste in useless imaginations and negative emotions, and wish to correct it as fast as possible. In what direction can I point my recovered energy?

A: But often, in the world's most crowded streets, but often, in the din of strife, there arises an unspeakable desire after the knowledge of our buried life; a thirst to spend our fire and restless force in tracking out our true, original course. (Arnold)

433. *Q*: And this, I believe, leads to genuine self-assurance?

A: Begin to search and dig in your own field for this pearl of eternity . . . and when you have found it you will know that all which you have sold or given away for it is as mere a nothing as a bubble upon the water. (Law)

Here is your fresh source of energy

434. *Q*: What is the meaning of the esoteric teaching that silence is strength?

A: True bravery is shown by performing without witness what one might be capable of doing before all the world. (La Rochefoucauld)

435. *Q*: The mystics speak of an inward friend who is more powerful than all exterior enemies. What do they mean by this?

A: Notwithstanding the sight of all those miseries which wring us, and threaten our destruction, we have still an instinct that we cannot repress, which elevates us above our sorrows. (Pascal)

436. *Q*: When our pain and panic reaches a crisis, the agony seems overwhelming. It is hard at these times to see how truth can conquer error.

A: I have often found a small stream at its source, that, when followed along its course, carried away the camel with its load. (Saadi)

437. *Q*: How can a person tell whether he is living from his true nature or from borrowed costumes?

A: What is not natively his own falls off and comes to nothing. (Landor)

438. *Q:* Why do we fail to use our minds with full power?

A: Every man takes the limits of his own field of vision for the limits of the world. (Schopenhauer)

439. *Q:* I have heard that true humility is the same thing as true strength, which I do not comprehend.

A: True piety has in it nothing weak, nothing sad, nothing constrained. It enlarges the heart; it is simple, free, and attractive. (Fénelon)

440. *Q:* More and more I see how we waste ourselves in shallow strivings, but I do not understand why we foolishly persist in them.

A: He who does not understand how the soul contains the Beautiful within itself, seeks to realize beauty without, by laborious production. (Plotinus)

441. *Q:* What a shocking but healthy discovery! I see clearly how personal weakness invites others to attempt to exploit and drain me.

A: To the generality of men you cannot give a stronger hint for them to impose upon you than by imposing upon yourself. (Fielding)

442. *Q:* I have a general sense of weariness in mind and spirit, which prevents me from giving much of myself to these studies. I need a fresh source of psychic power.

A: This energy does not descend into individual life on any other condition than entire possession. It comes to the lowly and simple; it comes to whomsoever will put off what is foreign and proud; it comes as insight; it comes as serenity and grandeur. (Emerson)

443. *Q:* The mystics teach the existence of great power within each man. Why, then, do we not see it?

A: It is true that all knowledge is within ourselves, but this has to be called forth by another knowledge. Although the capacity to know is inside us, it must be called out. (Vivekananda)

Understand this great cosmic law

444. Q: What can a person do if he feels that his habitual and traditional religion has failed him?

A: Freedom is a new religion. (Heine)

445. Q: People feel helplessly whirled about by the existing social structure, with its burdensome laws and taxes, crimes and uncertainties. What declaration of independence can be given to those who feel caught in the whirlpool?

A: If you did not desire your present position, you would not be doing everything possible to maintain it . . . If you cease doing those things which maintain your position, you will lose at once that position which you claim is forced upon you and which is your burden . . . It is impossible for any man to be placed against his own will in a condition which is contrary to his conscience. (Tolstoy)

446. Q: Why are we so doubtful about our possibilities for attaining a totally new life?

A: We know what we are, but not what we may be. (Shakespeare)

447. Q: We are told that a healthy but unseen work goes on within us as we collect information about cosmic matters. Please explain this secret work by facts.

A: We are weaving them into a unity, supplying to merely isolated things the hidden link of spiritual continuity and coherence, penetrating beneath the outward husk of facts to a something deeper, richer, more permanent. (Caird)

448. Q: Where can we start to understand some of the great cosmic laws which run the universe?

A: It is the spiritual always which determines the material. (Carlyle)

449. Q: I want to work hard on all this, so what must I personally contribute to these instructions in order to change them into beneficial experiences?

A: When moral courage feels that it is in the right, there is no personal daring of which it is incapable. (Hunt)

450. *Q*: What do we need to know about the nature of true self-strength?

A: It is the greatest manifestation of power to be calm. It is easy to be active. Let the reins go, and the horses will drag you down. Any one can do that, but he who can stop the plunging horses is the strong man. Which requires the greater strength, letting go, or restraining? The calm man is not the man who is dull ... Activity is the manifestation of the lower strength, calmness of the superior strength. (Vivekananda)

451. *Q*: I would like to persuade myself of the futility of putting off the spiritual adventure any longer.

A: We must fight the fight! ... We only find rest in effort. (Amiel)

452. *Q*: What is an example of a right and courageous viewpoint towards finding the new life?

A: We have both heard and believe that there is such a place to be found. (Bunyan)

Special paths to self-confidence

a. Self-strength comes from self-awareness, self-unity.
b. As we abandon false strength, true power appears.
c. You have the power to not be victimized by anyone.
d. Authentic self-confidence is always calm, never agitated.
e. Return to your natural state of dynamic living.
f. Courage comes by associating with cosmic facts.
g. Depend upon your own resources, not upon others.
h. Never permit others to drain your psychic energies.
i. Allow these principles to banish all self-doubt.
j. True self-power can never be stolen nor exhausted!

7. You Can Make Problems Disappear for Ever

453. *Q*: What is the basic cause of all our problems?

A: There are people in the world, who, having renounced all the laws of God and nature, have made laws for themselves which they strictly obey. (Pascal)

454. *Q*: Nothing has ever given me more encouragement than these ideas, but I wonder whether they can solve my particular problem, which I prefer not to identify.

A: There is a remedy for every wrong and a satisfaction for every soul. (Emerson)

455. *Q*: May I have a basic principle of guidance for avoiding problems with relatives?

A: Take precautions before the evil appears; regulate things before disorder has begun. (Lao-tse)

456. *Q*: Please explain how an inner wrongness creates an outer problem. It might motivate us towards self-elevation!

A: Nothing is a greater barrier to being on good terms with others than being ill at ease with yourself. (Balzac)

457. *Q*: Apparently we use the wrong tool in trying to solve our problems. Please identify a wrong tool.

A: He employs his emotion who can make no use of his reason. (Cicero)

458. *Q*: What is a specific example of a wrong emotion?

A: There is no passion that so much transports men from their right judgment as anger. (Montaigne)

459. *Q*: Anger is a major problem with most of us, even more so because we keep this particular emotion well concealed. Do you have suggestions for dealing with other people with calm and poise?

A: If you want your judgment to be accepted, express it coolly and without passion. All violence has its origin in the *will,* and so, if your judgment is expressed with vehemence, people will consider it an effort of will, and not the outcome of knowledge, which is in its nature calm and unemotional. (Schopenhauer)

460. *Q*: Nervousness is also a troublesome emotion with many people. We are nervous over money and health and politics and everything else. What can settle us down?

A: True philosophy is that which renders us to ourselves, and all others who surround us, better, and at the same time more content, more patient, more calm, and more ready for all decent and pure enjoyment. (Lavater)

461. *Q*: It is obvious that mankind never really solves its problems, but only rearranges them. Why don't men see that the only true solution is in this new and higher way of thinking?

A: You cannot talk to a summer insect about ice. (Zen)

Remedies are always within reach

462. *Q*: Our class in esotericism will be taking up a problem which awakened men mention quite often, that of false goodness. May I have an example of how a wrong sense of goodness bounces back as trouble?

A: Never try to please an envious person. (Vauvenargues)

463. *Q*: There are as many personal problems as stars!

Where can we find the time and energy to take up each one at a time and give it our earnest attention?

A: It matters not what our evils are ... hardness of heart, covetousness, wrath, pride, and ambition, etc., our remedy is always one and the same, always at hand, always certain and infallible. (Law)

464. *Q:* Please explain the remedy.

A: It is in the recognition or non-recognition of these principles that a man finds or fails to find freedom. (Tolstoy)

465. *Q:* What if we are visited by trouble while still not understanding the truths that could rescue us?

A: That which you do not understand when you read, you will understand in the day of your visitation, for many secrets of religion are not perceived till they be felt, and are not felt but in the day of calamity. (Taylor)

466. *Q:* I am tired of being told how I *should* behave. If we have duties to perform in life, they must certainly have nothing to do with hypocritical moral codes invented by pious frauds.

A: In society as it is now constituted, all the established rules are so many mechanical duties, while real duty consists in obeying the laws of our own being. (Cherbuliez)

467. *Q:* Maybe I am getting a bit of wisdom after all, for I suspect that I may be the cause of the troubles I get. What spiritual law explains this?

A: With what measure ye mete, it shall be measured to you again. (Jesus)

468. *Q:* So the punishments we get from others always start with some unconscious error in ourselves?

A: You cannot do wrong without suffering wrong. (Emerson)

469. *Q:* I have an important business project which I must

put into the hands of a responsible man. How can I estimate the reliability of several prospective employees?

A: A man shows his character just in the way in which he deals with trifles — for then he is off his guard. This will often afford a good opportunity of observing the boundless egoism of a man's nature, and his total lack of consideration for others; and if these defects show themselves in small things, or merely in his general manner, you will find that they also underlie his action in matters of importance, although he may disguise the fact . . . Do not trust him beyond your door. (Schopenhauer)

Love and wisdom must go together

470. *Q*: What sort of battle-cry can turn the power of our emotions into allies against misfortune?

A: I love everything, and dislike one thing only — the desperate imprisonment of my being . . , Liberty for the inner man is then the strongest of my passions — perhaps my only passion. (Amiel)

471. *Q*: What can we do about an adverse fate?

A: The fault . . . is not in our stars, but in ourselves. (Shakespeare)

472. *Q*: Can we safely let our conscience be our guide?

A: What we call conscience, is, in many instances, only a wholesome fear of the constable. (Bovee)

473. *Q*: Because they are unusual men, the mystic masters must have unusual ways to communicate their help to pupils. Correct?

A: One of the most wonderful things in nature is a glance; it transcends speech; it is the bodily symbol of identity. (Emerson)

474. *Q*: Why do the wise men of all philosophies advise us to keep our self-work to ourselves, and not even mention it to most people!

A: That conduct sometimes seems useless in the eyes of the world, the secret reasons for which, may, in reality, be wise and solid. (La Rochefoucauld)

475. *Q*: I would like to learn to enjoy each separate moment.

A: Peace of mind! That is something essential to any enjoyment of the present moment, and unless its separate moments are enjoyed, there is an end to life's happiness as a whole. We should always recollect that today comes only once, and never returns. We fancy that it will come again tomorrow, but tomorrow is another day, which, in its turn, comes once only.(Schopenhauer)

476. *Q*: You teach that wisdom must be mixed in with our love. Will you please explain what you mean?

A: Forgiveness is commendable, but apply not ointment to the wound of an oppressor. (Saadi)

477. *Q*: Most of us have so very little to contribute to our own self-transformation.

A: No heart that holds one right desire treads the road of loss. *(Bhagavad-Gita)*

478. *Q*: The mystic philosophers teach that a problem cannot be solved on its own level. What does that mean?

A: Nothing does so establish the mind amidst the rollings and turbulence of present things, as a look above them and a look beyond them, — above them, to the steady and good hand by which they are ruled, and beyond them, to the sweet and beautiful end to which, by that hand, they will be brought. (Taylor)

How to dissolve difficulties by relaxing

479. *Q*: In my present perplexity, I am faced with four different choices of possible solutions. How can I know which one is best for me?

A: As long as you lack self-unity, what difference does it make what you decide to do? (Sufism)

480. *Q*: Does this mean that the irritating problem of indecision arises because we are in self-contradiction, because a wall of illusion stands between us and reality?

A: To be upset at anything which happens to us is a separation of ourselves from nature. (Aurelius)

481. *Q*: What part does chance play in our lives? How can we command it for our best interests?

A: Chance will not do the work — chance sends the breeze; but if the pilot slumber at the helm, the very wind that wafts us towards the port may dash us on the shelves. The steersman's part is vigilance, blow it rough or smooth. (Scott)

482. *Q*: I think most of all we need deliverance from shallow platitudes and stupid sentimentalities about all the nice people who will help us with our problems.

A: A friend in need, as the saying goes, is rare. No, it is just the opposite; no sooner have you made a friend than he is in need and asks you for a loan. (Schopenhauer)

483. *Q*: We are taught to *stop* doing things, instead of trying to do, that is, to stop acting from false ideas and from artificial personality traits. What is the purpose of this technique?

A: Cease striving; then there will be self-transformation. (Chuang-tse)

484. *Q*: What is the healthy answer to the problem of extravagance, to wanting and buying things that won't add an inch to our contentment?

A: The man is richest whose pleasures are the cheapest. (Thoreau)

485. *Q*: We are advised to use the faults of others as lessons for self-maturity. Will you detail one such lesson?

A: When people are overcome by rage, it is good to observe attentively the effects on those who deliver themselves up to this emotion. (Plutarch)

486. *Q*: I have noticed both in myself and in others how many problems are caused by our desperate attempts to be noticed, to appear important, to feel respected and admired. What is the answer to this painful compulsion?

A: It is not at all necessary to be great, as long as we are in harmony with the order of the universe. (Amiel)

487. *Q*: But human power confers respect.

A: Those he commands, move only in command, nothing in love. (Shakespeare)

Why we run into unexpected disasters

488. *Q*: What could I say to a person who complains bitterly at the way life has treated him? He demands rewards and comforts from the people he blames for his misery. Perhaps a simple truth can penetrate his mind.

A: Nothing can bring you peace but yourself. Nothing can bring you peace but the triumph of principles. (Emerson)

489. *Q*: My problem has been with me for a long time. It is easier for me to be a good friend to others than to myself!

A: What is your aim? To be good? And how is this accomplished except by general principles, some about the nature of the universe, and others about the proper constitution of man. (Aurelius)

490. *Q*: I have noticed a particular form of anxiety in me, which is the worry that I may lose various items I have acquired through hard work.

A: Truth is the highest thing that man may keep. (Chaucer)

491. *Q*: Where do talents and gifts play their part in problem-solving?

A: Desire spiritual gifts. (New Testament)

492. *Q*: If I could hear the answer to this one question I could spend months thinking about it. The question is, why do we suddenly run into difficulties and disasters which give no visible warning?

A: We run carelessly to the cliff, after we have put something before us to prevent us seeing it. (Pascal)

493. *Q*: It seems that a wholehearted effort towards self-transformation would stir things up on the inside. What is the practical value in this?

A: When the fight begins within himself, a man's worth something. (Browning)

494. *Q*: I am puzzled by the esoteric teaching about inaction. The mystics state that the right kind of inaction is authentic action which transforms everything into its naturally healthy condition. But how can doing *nothing* produce *something*?

A: Who is there who can make muddy waters clear? But if allowed to remain still, it will gradually clear itself. (Lao-tse)

495. *Q*: May we have a few facts about inner guidance?

A: All our progress is an unfolding, like the vegetable bud. You have first an instinct, then an opinion, then a knowledge, as the plant has root, bud, and fruit. Trust the instinct to the end, though you can render no reason. (Emerson)

496. *Q*: You say that we make authentic gain by first experiencing a loss. Will you provide an example of this basic teaching?

A: It is only after a man has rid himself of all pretence, and taken refuge in mere unembellished existence, that he is able to attain that peace of mind which is the foundation of human happiness. (Schopenhauer)

Only consciousness can banish conflicts

497. *Q*: Eastern wise men teach that harmony with nature – including our own nature – delivers us from daily pain and frustration. What does this mean?

A: Is there any cause in nature that makes these hard hearts? (Shakespeare)

498. *Q*: Our study group consists of lawyers, real estate agents, and other men and women engaged in various businesses. We have been seeking the one key which reveals what we should do for ourselves as we go about our business duties. We want to wake up!

A: Our individual life consists in separating ourselves from our surroundings; in so reacting upon it that we apprehend it consciously, and make ourselves spiritual personalities – that is to say, intelligent and free. (Amiel)

499. *Q*: I do not understand why you say we must become clearly conscious of our problems. If we are unaware of them, they cannot bother us.

A: A stone beneath the surface of the ground is just as heavy as a visible one. (Eckhart)

500. *Q*: As one road to self-freedom, you have urged us to observe ourselves, to detect our hidden motives for doing what we do. May we hear of a specific area for self-observation?

A: We oftener says things because we can say them well, than because they are sound and reasonable. (Landor)

501. *Q*: I have a problem in deciding how to think correctly towards people in trouble. While feeling sympathy, I also sense that they have shirked their responsibilities towards themselves.

A: We may be pretty certain that persons whom all the world treats ill deserve entirely the treatment they get. The world is a looking-glass, and gives back to every man the reflection of his own face. Frown at it, and it will in turn look sourly upon you; laugh at it and with it, and it is a jolly, kind companion. (Thackeray)

502. *Q*: Is this the same as saying that we attract more of what we already are, that we receive exactly what our actual nature asks for?

A: Every man stamps his value on himself. The price we set for ourselves is given us . . . Man is made great or small by his own will. (Schiller)

503. *Q*: I need to see more clearly how I am punished by my own wrong attitude towards life.

A: He that will keep a monkey should pay for the glasses he breaks. (Selden)

504. *Q*: What is the correct attitude to have towards blundering mankind as a whole?

A: I have earnestly endeavoured not to laugh at human actions, nor to lament them, but to understand them. (Spinoza)

The value of spiritual exercises

505. *Q*: I have carried out these spiritual exercises with excellent results. For one thing, I see the value of reading with a relaxed and an enjoyable state of mind.

A: I would study, I would know, I would admire for ever. These works of thought have been the entertainments of the human spirit in all ages. (Emerson)

506. *Q*: There are thousands of puzzles and problems to be solved in the world of human events. Some of them seem so stubborn that I wonder if any personal effort can cut a man loose.

A: Truly, I see he that will but stand to the truth, it will carry him out. (Fox)

507. *Q*: Why are the most useless people always those who are the most noisy and demanding?

A: It is difficult to keep quiet if you have nothing to do. (Schopenhauer)

508. *Q*: I have a strange contradiction. Sometimes I am very grateful to others for benefiting me, but at other times I resent them for their benefits. I think I dislike feeling obligated to people.

A: Happy the man to whom Heaven has given a morsel of bread without laying him under the obligation of thanking any other for it than Heaven itself. (Cervantes)

509. *Q*: My need is for information. In analysing my self-invited battles, I find many of them occur because of my loneliness. It drives me into associations with people whom I sense are loaded with concealed cunning and hostility, but I blunder straight ahead anyway.

A: Those who have resources within themselves, who can dare to live alone, want friends the least, but, at the same time, best know how to prize them the most. But no company is far preferable to bad, because we are more apt to catch the vices of others than their virtues. (Colton)

510. *Q*: Why is it several people can have entirely different reactions to the same event, one responding with amusement, another in disappointment, a third with surprise?

A: Each one sees what he carries in his heart. (Goethe)

511. *Q*: It is said that love conquers all, so can it conquer all that is wrong with us?

A: Love is the crowning grace of humanity, the holiest right of the soul, the golden link which binds us to duty and truth, the redeeming principle that chiefly reconciles the heart to life, and is prophetic of eternal good. (Petrarch)

512. *Q*: What is a major turning point in our upward climb?

A: While we are aware of thirsting after knowledge, we

begin to seek here and there, wherever we think we can get some truth, and, failing to find it we become dissatisfied and seek in a fresh direction. All search is vain, until we begin to perceive that knowledge is within ourselves . . . that we must help ourselves . . . Then we may know that the sun is rising, that the morning is breaking for us, and, taking courage, we must persevere until the goal is reached. (Vivekananda)

513. *Q*: When I think of the many kinds of discontent which we must combat, I feel the need for a basic strategy.

   A: Who conquers indolence will conquer all the rest. (Lavater)

514. *Q*: I can see where we can use these ideas in many instances, like overcoming shyness, but I wonder how they might work in an especially tough situation? Just now I am faced with a crisis regarding my love life.

   A: Philosophy is the art and law of life, and it teaches us what to do in all cases, and, like good marksmen, to hit the target at any distance. (Seneca)

515. *Q*: Of all these ideas, the adventure of winning a new command over my own thoughts and feelings is the most interesting. I can think of nothing more practical than this.

   A: He who would be master of himself shall win it, if he bravely strives. *(Bhagavad-Gita)*

Your esoteric work is truly right!

516. *Q*: I have begun my mental life all over again, from the very start, just as if I knew nothing at all. At first I thought this represented weakness, but now I find it to be a source of new energy.

   A: When we begin at the real beginning – when thought starts where alone it legitimately can start – it is forced onwards, from step to step, by an irresistible inward necessity, and cannot stop short till it has found its goal in the sphere of universal and absolute truth, or in that Infinite Mind which is at once the beginning and the end, the source and the final explanation of all thought and being. (Caird)

517. Q: How does a mystic master meet the same problems we have?

A: I am too high for fortune to harm me. (Ovid)

518. Q: I was once told that I must have as much knowledge about what is wrong as I have knowledge of what is right. Why is it not enough to simply know what is right?

A: The knowledge of God without that of man's misery causes pride. The knowledge of man's misery without that of God causes despair. (Pascal)

519. Q: Where do people go wrong in thinking about God, Truth, Reality?

A: An idea about God is not God. (Tolstoy)

520. Q: My question is about rewards. While I know we are working for inner benefits, not for material rewards, I sometimes wonder whether I am gaining anything at all.

A: There is a third silent party to all our bargains. The nature and soul of things takes on itself the guaranty of the fulfilment of every contract, so that honest service cannot come to loss. If you serve an ungrateful master, serve him the more. Put God in your debt. Every stroke shall be repaid. The longer the payment is withholden, the better for you; for compound interest on compound interest is the rate and usage of this exchequer. (Emerson)

521. Q: Please show us how weakness and fear go together.

A: Weak people prefer to be dependent in order to be protected. Those who fear men love the laws of the land. (Vauvenargues)

522. Q: It would be interesting to hear how we will see the world when we have dissolved the mental mists as others have done.

A: The philosopher laughs, for he alone escapes being

duped, while he sees other men the victims of persistent illusion. He is like some mischievous spectator of a ball who has cleverly taken all the strings from the violins, and yet sees musicians and dancers moving and pirouetting before him as though the music were still going on. (Amiel)

523. Q: What would indicate that we are really dissolving our problems, instead of merely rearranging them?

A: A sound direction is not so much indicated by never making a mistake, as by never repeating it. (Bovee)

524. Q: How do we lose our natural power to solve problems and how can we regain it?

A: Every reaction in the form of hatred or evil is so much loss to the mind, and every evil thought or deed or hatred, or any thought of reaction, if it is controlled, will be laid in our favour. It is not that we lose by thus restraining ourselves; we are gaining infinitely more than we suspect . . . it is so much good energy stored up in our favour; that piece of energy will be converted into the higher powers. (Vivekananda)

525. Q: I simply have the feeling that our work with these ideas is *right* — that the richer life is a certainty.

A: Press on! A better fate awaits you. (Hugo)

Reflect upon these vital thoughts

a. Every problem and every conflict has a solution.
b. All answers exist in a clear and a calm mind.
c. We are both the cause and the cure of our difficulties.
d. If you deeply wish to abolish strife, you can do so.
e. A self-harmonious nature does not create problems.
f. Use your losses as lessons in living a free life.
g. As a crisis rises to consciousness, it begins to fade.
h. Do not have a fondness for habitual, but useless, ideas.
i. Work diligently at self-insight and self-understanding.
j. Realize that your esoteric efforts are truly right!

8. Secrets of Self-freedom and Self-command

526. *Q*: Where do we start our quest for freedom and independence?

A: Thought takes a man out of servitude into freedom. (Emerson)

527. *Q*: You refer, I believe, to the new thought aroused by a strong wish to break out of the old ways?

A: He is the free man whom the truth makes free, and all are slaves besides. (Cowper)

528. *Q*: I wonder whether other people have the same timidity that I have regarding independence? I mean that it sometimes seems frightening to break out of the social net to stand all alone.

A: I exist as I am — that is enough; if no other in the world be aware, I sit content. (Whitman)

529. *Q*: I sense the folly of depending upon others, so would appreciate counsel for breaking away.

A: If a man comes to think that I am more dependent upon him than he is dependent upon me, he feels as though I had stolen something from him, and his aim will be to have revenge and get it back. The only way to obtain superiority in dealing with men is to let it be seen that you are independent of them. (Schopenhauer)

530. *Q*: What do we need to know about self-slavery?

A: I will have care of being a slave to myself, for it is a perpetual, a humiliating, and the heaviest of all servitudes. Liberty is maintained by moderate desires. (Seneca)

531. *Q*: Are you saying that we can be entirely independent of fright and harm from events and objects in the exterior world? How?

A: Things stand outside us, themselves by themselves, neither knowing anything of themselves, nor expressing any judgment. What is it, then, which makes judgment about them? Your ruling faculty. (Aurelius)

532. *Q*: What do you mean by personal freedom?

A: Is freedom anything else than the power of living as we choose? Nothing else. Tell me then, you men, do you wish to live in error? We do not. No one who lives in error is free. Do you wish to live in fear? Do you wish to live in sorrow? Do you wish to live in tension? By no means. No one who is in a state of fear or sorrow or tension is free, but whoever is delivered from sorrows or fears or anxieties, he is at the same time also delivered from servitude. (Epictetus)

533. *Q*: You make it clear that freedom is the power to live as we choose, which is an attractive principle. Tell us of a good choice to make right now.

A: I prefer those men of genius who awaken in me the sense of truth, and who increase the sum of one's inner liberty. (Amiel)

How to maintain total self-command

534. *Q*: I am in conflict over the possibility of losing part of my financial security. Can these lessons teach me to remain calmly unaffected about such things?

A: Every mind seems capable of entertaining a certain quantity of happiness, which no institutions can increase, no circumstances alter, and entirely independent of fortune. (Goldsmith)

535. *Q*: Then through right self-work we can win command

over our circumstances, regardless of their nagging nature?

A: Self-control, too, is something which we have in our own power. (Schopenhauer)

536. *Q*: To me, freedom means freedom from neurosis, unhappiness, and hostility. By this standard, few live in freedom, though everyone claims to love it.

A: None are more hopelessly enslaved than those who falsely believe they are free. (Goethe)

537. *Q*: Am I correct in defining freedom as an absence of worry and hostility?

A: Who then is free? The wise man who can govern himself. (Horace)

538. *Q*: Beneath all our pretense of gaiety, we sense our slavery to our unfaced problems. What prevents us from rising up in a mighty rebellion to throw it off?

A: So helpless does slavery make men that they grow fond of it. (Vauvenargues)

539. *Q*: Please give us a starting point for overthrowing the common human weakness for flattery.

A: Do you wish to be praised by a man who curses himself three times an hour? Do you wish to please a man who cannot please himself? (Aurelius)

540. *Q*: The great avatars teach that the truth is deeply hidden within us, needing only our invitation to grow and burst our chains. Please describe this process.

A: Truth comes home to the mind so naturally that when we learn it for the first time, it seems as though we do no more than recall it to our memory. (Fontenelle)

541. *Q*: Thanks to these principles, I now see that the more the public applauds an action, the more wrong the action may be.

A: All creatures live bewildered, save some few. *(Bhagavad-Gita)*

542. *Q*: That is a perfect reason for resolving to live with an independent mind.

A: He who hangs on to the errors of the ignorant multitude, must not be counted among the great men. (Cicero)

543. *Q*: Why do we fail to see false ideas as false?

A: Hardly one in ten thousand will have the strength of mind to ask himself seriously and earnestly, 'Is that true?' (Schopenhauer)

Self-liberty is your natural state

544. *Q*: Since human beings falsify everything, what is their counterfeit version of freedom?

A: None can love freedom heartily, but good men; the rest love not freedom, but licence. (Milton)

545. *Q*: I am now aware of how society is caught in its own web, but I hope that the individual who wants to escape can still do so.

A: Before man made us citizens, great Nature made us men. (Lowell)

546. *Q*: Then self-knowledge is the way to self-freedom?

A: Chief among the causes of liberty is devotion, the watchfulness of the spirit towards its own nature. (Shankara)

547. *Q*: So we surround ourselves by psychic prison bars by our failure to study the ways we think and act?

A: In living creatures, ignorance of self is nature; in man it is a vice. (Boethius)

548. *Q*: You say that gullibility is a chain which most people wear without even feeling it. No doubt this is true of

me, so what information about human nature can help break the chain?

A: What appears to be generosity is usually nothing more than disguised ambition, which despises petty self-interests in order to gain greater self-interests. (La Rochefoucauld)

549. *Q*: Now that I understand how man preys upon man, I also understand something else, which at first is startling. Society publicly praises individuality and independence, but really fears those who stand on their own feet.

A: Society everywhere is in conspiracy against the manhood of every one of its members . . . Self-reliance is its aversion. (Emerson)

550. *Q*: I want to be a self-directed man. How?

A: Eagles fly alone; they are but sheep which always herd together. (Sidney)

551. *Q*: But isn't it right and necessary to have various kinds of authorities? Don't they do their best to make us secure and comfortable?

A: Are you less a slave by being loved and favoured by your master? . . . Your master favours you; he will soon beat you. (Pascal)

552. *Q*: I have met a few men who have attained self-command to one degree or another. I have noticed that the higher his level, the less pretence and the more authentic pleasantness.

A: Good sense and good-nature are never separated, though the ignorant world has thought otherwise. Good nature, by which I mean beneficence and candour, is the product of right reason. (Dryden)

553. *Q*: What sort of self-effort really makes a difference?

A: Great thoughts reduced to practice become great acts. (Hazlitt)

554. Q: I lose my self-command whenever I feel offended, though I usually keep it hidden from others. How can I change this?

A: Remember that it is not the man who gives blows or abuse who offends you, but the view you take of these things as being offensive. When, therefore, anyone provokes you, be assured that it is your own opinion which provokes you. (Epictetus)

Give a wide welcome to higher impressions

555. Q: My first steps away from my old nature must be very short ones, so may I have a suitable thought?

A: Our greatest glory consists not in never falling, but in rising every time we fall. (Goldsmith)

556. Q: What is our personal responsibility in achieving self-liberty?

A: Liberty in submission — what a problem! And yet that is what we must always come back to. (Amiel)

557. Q: May we hear more about this correct and beneficial submission? To what do we submit ourselves?

A: Our activity should consist in placing ourselves in a state of susceptibility to Divine impressions, and pliability to all the operations of the Eternal Word. (Guyon)

558. Q: I wish to have this more abundant life.

A: All we have to do is to receive what we are given (de Caussade)

559. Q: But what if I lack the necessary strong belief to bring this newness to me?

A: Belief consists in accepting the affirmations of the soul; unbelief, in denying them. (Emerson)

560. Q: How can I maintain a pleasant nature, not merely when things are going my way, but at all times?

A : Your disposition will be suitable to that which you most frequently think about, for the spirit is, as it were, tinged with the colour and complexion of its own thoughts. (Aurelius)

561. *Q*: I am especially interested in understanding how inward victory expands itself to outward triumph. May I have a thought on this?

A : If you are inwardly free from fighting, no one will be able to fight with you. (Taoism)

562. *Q*: What about those times when we feel battered by the world?

A : Truth is tough. It will not break, like a bubble, at a touch . . . you may kick it about all day, like a football, and it will be round and full at evening. (Holmes)

563. *Q*: I was first attracted to these principles by seeing how easily we can lose those liberties which are based on human plans. Only the spiritual is secure.

A : Let me tell you, that as here lies all the true and real freedom, which cannot be taken from you, so in the constant exercise of this freedom, that is, in a continual leaving yourself to, and depending upon the operation of God in your soul, lies all your road to heaven. No divine virtue can be had any other way. (Law)

564. *Q*: What is the esoteric teaching about worship?

A : Better than worshipping gods is obedience to the laws of righteousness. (Buddha)

New thoughts lead to new independence

565. *Q*: Since our life is what our thoughts make it, what kind of thoughts lead a man back to his natural independence?

A : His individual dignity, not derived from birth, from success, from wealth, from outward show, but consisting in the indestructible principles of his soul – this ought to enter into his habitual consciousness. (Channing)

566. Q: It was a surprising revelation, but you have made me conscious of my dependence upon borrowed ideas — most of them false. I wish to toss out this dependency once and for all.

A: They who have light in themselves will not revolve as satellites. (Seneca)

567. Q: What is the alternative to relying upon the notions we have picked up from the past?

A: Rely on principles. (Epictetus)

568. Q: A group of us have determined to no longer hear merely what we prefer to hear, but will listen to whatever is truly good for us, regardless of our tender feelings. Will you please give us a challenging truth to face?

A: One would be apt to think, from the murmurs of impatient mortals, that God owed them a recompense before they had deserved it, and that he was obliged to reward their virtue beforehand. No, let us first be virtuous, and rest assured we shall sooner or later be happy. Let us not require the prize before we have won the victory. (Rousseau)

569. Q: Please give us a specific instance of where society defeats its own search for freedom.

A: Hero-worship is strongest where there is the least regard for human freedom. (Spencer)

570. Q: You say that the false must go before the true can come. What particular falseness can we work against in order to find self-release?

A: Every man's nature is concealed with many folds of disguise, and covered with various veils. His brows, his eyes, and very often his countenance, are deceitful, and his speech is most commonly a lie. (Cicero)

571. *Q*: I now see that the so-called easy way of behaving like a social sheep is the hard way after all. I want to be my own man.

A: It is easy in the world to live after the world's opinion; it is easy in solitude to live after your own; but the great man is he who, in the midst of the crowd, keeps with perfect sweetness the independence of solitude. (Emerson)

572. *Q*: I still do not understand why our thinking should not simply fall in with the majority. That seems to be the best we can do in this ailing world.

A: Why do we follow the majority? Is it because they have more reason? No, because they have more power. (Pascal)

Your genuine needs are always supplied

573. *Q*: Mine is a familiar question about self-independence, but the answer is not so easily found. Is there a method by which I can learn to cast aside my artificial personality traits and to simply be myself?

A: A man can be *himself* only so long as he is alone, and if he does not love solitude, he will not love freedom, for it is only when he is alone that he is really free. Restraint is always present in society, like a companion of whom there is no riddance, and in proportion to the greatness of a man's individuality, it will be hard for him to bear the sacrifices which all contact with others demands. (Schopenhauer)

574. *Q*: What information could free a man obsessed with the desire to expand his world at the cost of personal peace?

A: A man's affections are just as fully satisfied by the smallest circle as they can be by a large circle. (Balzac)

575. *Q*: We seem to trade our integrity for things we assume that we need, as when we please people so that they will also be pleased with us. Does our ascent to higher levels of consciousness supply our genuine needs?

A: In all places where you shall come, you will find no want at all. (Bunyan)

576. *Q*: In a single sentence, how can we be in charge of everything that happens to us, whether good or bad?

A: Philosophy alone makes the mind invincible and places us out of the reach of fortune, so that all her arrows fall short of us. (Seneca)

577. *Q*: We have learned about many of our wrong wishes, so please next give us a right wish.

A: I wish to be a true and free man. (Emerson)

578. *Q*: How can we become true men?

A: Great men are the true men, the men in whom Nature has succeeded. (Amiel)

579. *Q*: It would be nice to feel that this is also possible for us.

A: All may do what has by man been done. (Young)

580. *Q*: As you have stated, this is a challenging task, but I know we have every reason to feel confident.

A: Be cheerful, also, and seek not external help, nor the peace which others give. A man must stand straight, and not be kept straight by others. (Aurelius)

581. *Q*: Please connect self-independence with self-happiness.

A: Himself is the source of the best and most a man can be or achieve. The more this is so — the more a man finds his sources of pleasure in himself — the happier he will be . . . For all other sources of happiness are in their nature most uncertain. (Schopenhauer)

582. *Q*: I have just started to read esoteric literature, and wish to proceed with the most beneficial attitude.

A. Read not to contradict and confute, nor to believe

and take for granted, nor to find talk and discourse, but to weigh and consider. (Bacon)

The fascination of esoteric studies!

583. *Q*: What basic rule will help us retain self-command when dealing with an angry person?

A: Oppose not rage while rage is in its force, but give it way a while and let it waste. (Shakespeare)

584. *Q*: You have explained that we can have a geniune positive attitude, based on reality, or a fictitious positive attitude, based on self-deception. Please comment on a false positiveness.

A: The most positive men are the most credulous, since they most believe themselves, and advise most with their falsest flatterer and worst enemy — their own self-love. (Pope)

585. *Q*: How can we have a genuinely positive mind?

A: Before God can deliver us from ourselves, we must undeceive ourselves. (Augustine)

586. *Q*: People are always setting up standards of conduct for other people, which usually reflect some kind of self-righteousness or self-interest. Show us how to live by our own rightness.

A: Whatever one does or says, I must be good, just as if the emerald were always saying, 'Whatever anyone does or says, I must be an emerald and keep my colour.' (Aurelius)

587. *Q*: I have learned that liberty of all kinds is preserved through alertness towards those who would cunningly steal it with gifts.

A: Liberty is of more value than any gifts, and to receive gifts from men is to lose it. Be assured that men most commonly seek to oblige you only that they may engage you to serve them. (Saadi)

588. *Q*: You pointed out that self-reliance is a stout shield against getting into trouble. May we have an instance of this?

A: I have often said that all the misfortunes of men spring from their not knowing how to live quietly at home, in their own rooms. (Pascal)

589. *Q*: Presently, my foremost attitude towards these lessons is one of growing interest, even towards those I do not fully understand. I am wondering what other attitudes will flow into us as we go on?

A: How our delight in any particular study, art, or science rises and improves in proportion to the application which we bestow upon it. Thus, what was at first an exercise becomes at length an entertainment. (Addison)

590. *Q*: What would be a good declaration for us to live by?

A: I will walk at liberty: for I seek thy precepts. (Old Testament)

591. *Q*: Please comment in general on freedom from anger.

A: When I am angry my whole mind has become a huge wave of anger. I feel it, see it, handle it, can easily manipulate it, can fight with it, but I shall not succeed perfectly in the fight until I can get down below. A man says something very harsh to me, and I begin to feel that I am getting heated, and he goes on till I am perfectly angry, and forget myself, identify myself with anger. When he first began to abuse me I still thought, 'I am going to be angry.' Anger was one thing and I was another, but when I became angry, I was anger. These feelings have to be controlled in the germ, the root, in their fine forms, before even we have become conscious that they are acting on us. (Vivekananda)

Make internal freedom your goal

592. *Q*: My friends sometimes ask me what esotericism is all about, which I explain in various ways. What might be a summarized explanation?

A: There is provided an escape from the narrowness and poverty of the individual life, and the possibility of a life which is other and larger than our own, and yet which is most truly our own. For, to be ourselves, we must be more than ourselves. What we call love is, in truth . . . the losing of our individual selves to gain a larger self. (Caird)

593. *Q*: Religions and philosophies teach that an enlightened man becomes his own law, which is truly right and moral, in contrast to man-made law. Is that what you mean by self-independence?

A: A heroic person walks at his ease through and out of that custom or precedent or authority that suits him not. (Whitman)

594. *Q*: How do you summarize the esoteric teaching regarding man-made rules and spiritual rules?

A: Love is the fulfilling of the law. (New Testament)

595. *Q*: It was both surprising and pleasing to hear that we can use every problem for greater freedom. How might I use verbal attacks from others?

A: Never disregard what your enemies say. They may be severe, they may be prejudiced, they may be determined to see only in one direction, but still in that direction they see clearly. They do not speak all the truth, but they generally speak the truth from one point of view; so far as that goes, attend to them. (Haydon)

596. *Q*: What is the right attitude to take towards a person who praises you one moment and threatens you the next?

A: The anger of an ape — the threat of a flatterer — these deserve equal regard. (Epictetus)

597. *Q*: I would be the happiest man on earth if I could cease to be a slave of my circumstances. What can the teachers of esotericism do for us in this trap?

A: The great make us feel, first of all, the indifference

of circumstances. They call into activity the higher perceptions, and subdue the low habits of comfort and luxury; but the higher perceptions find their objects everywhere; only the low habits need palaces and banquets. (Emerson)

598. *Q*: I need to discover freedom from a tense self-defensiveness, which leaves me exhausted at the end of the day.

A: Dwelling in the light, there is no occasion at all for stumbling, for all things are discovered in the light. (Fox)

599. *Q*: People often feel that the Higher Power has placed us in this world without sufficient strength and aid.

A: He has delivered you into your own care, and says, 'I had no one better to entrust him to than yourself. Keep him for me, such as he is by nature — modest, faithful, upright, unafraid, free from passion and dread.' (Epictetus)

600. *Q*: What is an example of a free mind?

A: True eloquence scorns eloquence. (Pascal)

601. *Q*: I wish to avoid unnecessary problems in my esoteric studies. What can remind me to remain constant and systematic?

A: He is unwise who looks at the fruit of lofty trees, but does not measure their height. (Quintus)

602. *Q*: My class is making progress with several elementary lessons on self-liberty, but may we also have a more difficult one for study?

A: The internal nature is much higher than the external, and much more difficult to grapple with, much more difficult to control; therefore he who has conquered the internal nature controls the whole universe; it becomes his servant. (Vivekananda)

603. *Q*: I sense the purity of purpose of a teacher of truth. How might he best express it in words?

A: I want to help you to grow as beautiful as God meant you to be when he thought of you first. (MacDonald)

The esoteric path to freedom

a. True freedom resides in a free mind and spirit.
b. You need not be chained by people or circumstances.
c. Choose self-command for yourself right now.
d. To be aware of non-liberty is the beginning of liberty.
e. Self-independence is your right and natural state.
f. Use self-reliance as a guiding light to inner peace.
g. The truth is stronger than any crisis or difficulty.
h. Authentic freedom can never be taken away from you.
i. Let truthful principles succeed within your mind.
j. Make your personal declaration of independence!

9. Here Is the Cure for Pain and Suffering

604. *Q*: Obviously, we must understand the nature of suffering if we are to dissolve it. Where can we start?

A: One must plunge into it, and I have done so. (Amiel)

605. *Q*: What kind of knowledge about sorrow sets us free from sorrow?

A: In the loss of an object we do not proportion our grief to its real value, but to the value our fancies set upon it. (Addison)

606. *Q*: That helpful information affirms our need for insight into the ways of the mind.

A: The price of wisdom is above rubies. (Old Testament)

607. *Q*: How would you describe man's present condition?

A: Man does not know in what rank to place himself. He has plainly gone astray, and fallen from his true place, without being able to find it again. He seeks it anxiously and unsuccessfully, everywhere in impenetrable darkness. (Pascal)

608. *Q*: How can we turn on our mental lanterns to full light?

A: Observe yourself as your greatest enemy would do; so shall you be your greatest friend. (Taylor)

609. *Q*: The one word that characterizes me best of all is

restlessness. I no sooner reach my desired destination than I want to roam to somewhere else. One minute I'm all excited over something and the next minute it bores me. What causes my dissatisfaction?

A: What do you suppose will satisfy the soul except to walk free and own no superior? (Whitman)

610. *Q*: I recently suffered severe humiliation in my relation with another person. Before meeting esotericism, I would have wanted revenge, but now I wish to use the experience for inner elevation. How?

A: How is inner unity even possible under such circumstances? . . . To be sure, the best thing he can do is to recognize which part of him smarts the most under defeat, and let it always gain the victory. This he will always be able to do by the use of his reason . . . Let him resolve of his own free will to undergo the pain which the defeat of the other part involves. This is character. (Schopenhauer)

611. *Q*: What is an example of a man's inner contradiction which punishes him because he fails to see it in himself?

A: I have often wondered how it is that every man loves himself more than all the rest of men, but yet sets less value on his own opinion of himself than on the opinion of others. (Aurelius)

612. *Q*: I would like to live in a simple contentment, but the urge for fame and fortune seems so rewarding.

A: He is well paid that is well satisfied. (Shakespeare)

The only solution to suffering

613. *Q*: What is your first principle for removing sorrowful experiences?

A: The first is by clearing of the understanding, thereto adding a supernatural light, by which natural reason comes to see something that it saw not before, or at least did not esteem before. (Baker)

614. *Q*: So we cause our own suffering by a refusal to listen to higher inspirations?

A: When the ship does not yield to the rudder, it yields to the rock. (France)

615. *Q*: Will you make the lesson about yielding and surrendering somewhat clearer?

A: It is right to yield to the truth. (Horace)

616. *Q*: So esoteric self-education is the only solution to pain?

A: Ignorance is the root of misfortune. (Plato)

617. *Q*: I have tried to explain to myself the hazards of self-ignorance, but have been unable to put it into a clear statement. Will you please do so?

A: Man is nothing but contradiction; the less he knows it the more dupe he is. (Amiel)

618. *Q*: But we can rise above this self-contradiction to our natural and peaceful state?

A: We live in succession, in division, in parts, in particles. Meantime within man is the soul of the whole; the wise silence; the universal beauty, to which every part and particle is equally related; the eternal One. (Emerson)

619. *Q*: I am beginning to see why the sages say that the worst deception is self-deception. Our proud insistence that we are living in a palace is the very fraud that keeps us in the dungeon.

A: Nothing is so easy as to deceive one's self, for what we wish to believe, we readily believe, but such expectations are often inconsistent with the real state of things. (Demosthenes)

620. *Q*: A friend has asked me a certain question about social chaos, which I will ask of you. How does individual irresponsibility expand itself to community calamity?

A: The common people are but ill judges of a man's merits; they are slaves to fame, and their eyes are dazzled with the pomp of titles and large retinue. No wonder, then, that they bestow their honours on those who least deserve them. (Horace)

621. *Q*: You have said that the thrill that men get by worldly success is always accompanied by feelings of guilt and despair. Why is this?

A: Because they cannot hope to rise except by frustrating one another. (Vauvenargues)

622. *Q*: I don't want to conquer the world; I just want to be contented with myself.

A: Remember that the ruling faculty is invincible; when self-collected it is satisfied with itself . . . therefore the mind which is free from passions is a citadel, for man has nothing more secure to which he can fly for safety. (Aurelius)

Study your heartache scientifically

623. *Q*: I am encouraged by a discovery I made in a book of deep wisdom. It said that new life can begin only when the pressure from frustration and despair reaches the cracking point. Does this mean that our cracking is a cracking *open*, that it is the very *exit* from our ego-prison?

A: It seldom happens that a man changes his life through his habitual reasoning. No matter how fully he may sense the new plans and aims revealed to him by reason, he continues to plod along in the old paths until his life becomes frustrating and unbearable . . . he finally makes the change only when his usual life can no longer be tolerated. (Tolstoy)

624. *Q*: That is an amazingly new way to look at suffering.

A: The eternal stars shine out as soon as it is dark enough. (Carlyle)

625. *Q*: But can we, with all our instabilities, grasp this?

A: You can understand this by giving careful attention to what has been said. *(Theologia Germanica)*

626. *Q*: A willingness to let go of all that we at present and falsely think is valuable, is the way to a self-success that satisfies. The way is not found elsewhere, such as in a scholarly education. Are my two statements correct?

A: This is every man's short lesson of life, and he that has well learned it, is scholar enough, and has had all the benefit of a most finished education. (Law)

627. *Q*: The lessons we have heard so far indicate that we can use our tribulations for self-freedom or for self-imprisonment, according to the way we handle them.

A: Sweet are the uses of adversity. (Shakespeare)

628. *Q*: What would be a wrong use of suffering?

A: It is dangerous to abandon one's self to the luxury of grief, for it deprives one of courage and even the wish for recovery. (Amiel)

629. *Q*: You seem to say that suffering can be studied scientifically, with profitable results.

A: This science is not theoretical, but practical, in which experience surpasses the most polished and clever speculation. (Molinos)

630. *Q*: Several of us in our study group have been helped by seeing the folly of wasting our time in the social beehive. Will you please make this even clearer to us?

A: The social impulse does not rest directly upon the love of people, but upon the fear of solitude. It is not just the charm of having the company of others that people seek; it is the dreary oppression of being alone — the monotony of their own consciousness — that they would avoid. They will do anything to escape it, even put up with bad companions, and tolerate the feeling of restraint which all society involves, which is very burdensome. (Schopenhauer)

631. *Q*: Insight into this is true wisdom?

A: Wisdom consist in performing only useful actions. (Cherbuliez)

How to cure yourself swiftly

632. *Q*: What is the correct way to sympathize with those in sorrow?

A: One should never be very forward in offering spiritual consolations to those in distress. These, to be of any service, must be self-evolved in the first instance. (Coleridge)

633. *Q*: We are cautioned against rising up with false elation, elation based on vanity or a feeling of superiority. How can we recognize this kind of artificial joy?

A: As high as we have mounted in delight, in our dejection do we sink as low. (Wordsworth)

634. *Q*: What kind of desire would dominate a mind which is marching towards mental health?

A: What is it that any thoughtful, serious men could wish for, but to have a new heart, and a new spirit, free from the hellish self-tormenting elements of selfishness, envy, pride and wrath? (Law)

635. *Q*: How are our receptive minds affected by the truths and principles we are hearing?

A: When the ripe moment comes, the truth within answers to the fact without, as the flower responds to the sun, giving it . . . heat and colour. (Mabie)

636. *Q*: Does this newness free us from any suffering which others may try to impose upon us?

A: The man who has no wound on his hand may touch poison with his hand, for poison cannot affect a man with no open wound. Neither is there evil for the man free of evil. (Buddhism)

637. *Q*: I feel it important to know more about the labels which people like to paint upon others, both flattering labels and slanderous ones.

A: I leave it to other people to call me this or that. It matters little what any one is *called*. (Macdonald)

638. *Q*: I have suffered several severe losses lately, including that of someone very close to me. I know it does no good to feel sorry for myself, so I don't fall into that trap. However, I would like to have the mystical explanation regarding personal loss.

A: Nothing is ever really lost, or can be lost, no birth, identity, form — no object in the world, nor life, nor any visible thing; appearance must not foil, nor shifted sphere confuse thy brain. Ample are time and space — ample the fields of Nature. (Whitman)

639. *Q*: How does this inner refreshment actually flow into us when we use grief correctly? Please provide an example.

A: When, in some dreadful and ghastly dream, we reach the moment of greatest horror, it awakes us; thereby banishing all the hideous shapes that were born of the night. And life is a dream: when the moment of greatest horror compels us to break it off, the same thing happens. (Thoreau)

640. Q: Suffering is no doubt an excellent teacher, when rightly used, but why do we so seldom use it correctly?

A: Few people are wise enough to prefer useful reproof to treacherous praise. (La Rochefoucauld)

There is a way out!

641. *Q*: Teachers like Krishnamurti and George Gurdjieff say that people falsely value their sufferings, which I have noticed in myself. Pains supply a strange excitement, a fiery agitation, which burns up true life. Please verify this.

A: There are moods in which we court suffering, in the hope that here, at least, we shall find reality, sharp peaks and edges of truth. But it turns out to be scene-painting and counterfeit. The only thing grief has taught me is to know how shallow it is. (Emerson)

642. Q: It was a strange discovery to me, but I now see that many people actually enjoy their suffering.

A: The wretched hasten to hear of their own miseries. (Seneca)

643. Q: What is their cure?

A: To learn to look away from oneself is necessary in order to see many things. (Nietzsche)

644. Q: There seems to be room for the right kind of defiance in the spiritual journey, not the angry kind, but one composed of the will to succeed against all foes. Comment, please.

A: Let fortune do her worst, whatever she makes us lose, so long as she never makes us lose our honesty and independence. (Pope)

645. Q: Will an understanding of these principles help me with a problem connected with the people with whom I work?

A: A free mind has power to achieve all things. (Eckhart)

646. Q: How can we see this newness in our daily lives?

A: Only that day dawns to which we are awake. (Thoreau)

647. Q: I am almost afraid to ask my question! Self-righteousness is my chief malady. What is your medicine?

A: Do you never look at yourself when you criticize another person? (Plautus)

648. Q: Since it is the truth that hurts, we must obviously enter into and pass beyond the hurt in order to grow. Will

you please supply a method for doing this?

A: We would gain more by letting ourselves be seen as we really are, than by attempting to appear what we are not. (La Rochefoucauld)

649. *Q*: That seems to call for courage to face things according to reality, not according to our imagination.

A: Fearless minds climb soonest unto crowns. (Shakespeare)

650. *Q*: What can we do about vague fears, I mean, the kind which we hardly recognize, and which seem to have no definite source?

A: He who has found the bliss of the Eternal has no fear from any quarter. *(Upanishads)*

651. *Q*: One member of our esoteric school suggested a basic practice to employ at all times, but especially with the approach of psychic storm clouds. He suggested that we simply remember that there is a way out, and that it can be found. Your comment, please?

A: Look at no inward or outward trouble in any other view; reject every other thought about it, and then every kind of trial and distress will become the blessed day of your property. (Law)

652. *Q*: But what if we cannot find this self-satisfying reality?

A: I laugh when I hear that the fish swimming in the water is thirsty. (Kabir)

How to escape self-imprisonment

653. *Q*: I would appreciate a comment about a lesson I heard recently. The lesson explained that only whatever is false in us can suffer, and that our true nature resembles pure air, which attacking arrows cannot strike because there is nothing there for them to strike.

A: The ruling faculty does not disturb itself, I mean, it does not frighten itself or cause itself pain . . . The guiding principle in itself wants nothing, unless it makes a want for itself, and therefore it is free. (Aurelius)

654.   *Q*: My inner life is so complicated!

A: Simplicity of character is the natural result of profound thought. (Hazlitt)

655.   *Q*: I have noticed that the sighting of an attractive object of any kind arouses my desire to possess it, which is then followed by the painful realization that I cannot have it. What can I do about this punishing mental process?

A: It is proof of great talents to recall the mind from the senses, and to separate thought from habit. (Cicero)

656.   *Q*: I need the help of something above myself.

A: The soul's communication of truth is the highest event in nature . . . and this communication is an influx of the Divine Mind into our mind . . . Every moment when the individual feels invaded by it is memorable. (Emerson)

657.   *Q*: But who can know this superior state?

A: The man who yearns to know. *(Bhagavad-Gita)*

658.   *Q*: Feelings of persecution seem to exist to one degree or another in many people. No doubt this is an unconscious source of suffering, which right thinking can erase.

A: A great spirit is above insult, injustice, grief, and mockery. (La Bruyère)

659.   *Q*: What could help a person who feels rejected by people because he was once in serious trouble with the law?

A: The mind alone cannot be exiled. (Ovid)

660.   *Q*: I am at present investigating the ways in which we place ourselves in psychic prison. Please mention one way.

A: The world is imprisoned by its own activity. (Hinduism)

661. *Q*: May I have the full details of this?

A: The man who spends his life in sensual acts performs acts that depend upon temporary causes beyond his control. Of himself he does nothing, but it seems to him that he is acting independently. In reality, all that he imagines he is doing by himself is done through him by a higher power; he is not the creator of life but its prisoner. But the man who devotes his life to the recognition and practice of the truth revealed to him unites himself with the source of universal life, and accomplishes not personal or individual acts that depend upon time and space, but acts that have no cause, but are in themselves causes of all else, and have an endless significance. (Tolstoy)

662. *Q*: What is the foundation of this true action?

A: Let your understanding be your action. (Kierkegaard)

The pleasures of your inner journey

663. *Q*: When it comes to unburdening myself from grief, I am like a man who tries to get rid of a heavy brick by shifting it from his left hand to his right! How can I drop it?

A: The being who has attained harmony, and every being may attain it, has found his place in the order of the universe, and represents the divine thought at least as clearly as a flower or a solar system. Harmony seeks nothing outside itself. It is what it ought to be; it is the expression of right, order, law, and truth; it is greater than time, and represents eternity. (Amiel)

664. *Q*: Please give us a cosmic law governing mental pain.

A: He who commits injustice is made more wretched than he who suffers it. (Plato)

665. *Q*: What would be an example of concealed mental cruelty between friends?

A: In the adversity of our best friends, we often find something which does not displease us. (La Rochefoucauld)

666. *Q*: My close observation of people has made one of your teachings very clear to me — the happiness of most people is nothing but a stage performance.

A: Most become so only through imitation, and deliberately counterfeit high spirits and cheerfulness. (Vauvenargues)

667. *Q*: When I look at the unthinking ways of men and women I can see what great patience the mystic masters must possess!

A: The work an unknown good man has done is like a vein of water flowing hidden underground, secretly making the ground green. (Carlyle)

668. *Q*: Why do so many people fail to find happiness?

A: All men wish to be happy, but are dull at perceiving exactly what it is that makes life happy. (Seneca)

669. *Q*: Will you please review and clarify what is necessary for personal peace?

A: Happiness is no other than soundness and perfection of the mind. (Aurelius)

670. *Q*: I would like to mention a pleasant experience I have had with these thoughts. At first I was timid towards them, then curious, then attracted, and finally captivated by their trueness and kindness.

A: Mental pleasures never clog; unlike those of the body, they are increased by repetition, approved of by reflection, and strengthened by enjoyment. (Colton)

671. *Q*: I do not understand the first principles about cosmic guidance. It seems to require the absence of self-will and self-contradiction, but I would value more information.

A: We are never without a pilot. When we know not

how to steer, and dare not hoist a sail, we can drift. The
current knows the way, though we do not. The ship of
heaven guides itself, and will not accept a wooden rudder.
(Emerson)

672. Q: Where does this reliance on natural currents take a
man?

A: He attains freedom from all worldly cares and
anxieties, and nothing can ever chain him again. (Ramakrishna)

A clear mind is a treasure

673. Q: You have repeatedly stated that the first step
towards freedom is to become aware of self-imprisonment,
which I now see as practical wisdom. Please mention one
prison cell occupied by unaware people.

A: What people will say — in these words there lies the
tyranny of the world, the whole destruction of our natural
disposition, the uneven vision of our minds. These four words
bear sway everywhere. (Auerbach)

674. Q: For a long time I have felt blackmailed by society,
especially in its demands that I approve its clownish hustle by
joining it. Lately, I have added another thought to this,
which is, I have permitted this blackmail by not living
according to honest principles.

A: He who floats with the current, who does not guide
himself according to higher principles, who has no ideal, no
convictions — such a man is . . . a thing moved, instead of a
living and moving being — an echo, not a voice. The man who
has no inner life is a slave of his surroundings, as the
barometer is the obedient servant of the air. (Amiel)

675. Q: This confirms the mystic teaching that we act
wrong because we are unable to recognize what is right.

A: Not to understand a treasure's worth . . . is cause of
half the poverty we feel, and makes the world the wilderness
it is. (Cowper)

676. *Q*: Please review an area where we have gone wrong, but which we can make right.

A: We are all taking that which is bad for that which is good, and that which is a dream for that which is real. Soul is the only reality, and we have forgotten it. (Vivekananda)

677. *Q*: I used to suffer intensely in my relations with the opposite sex, which I thought were based in love. But now I am conscious of an esoteric truth which I refused to face for many years, which says that false love quickly turns to hate. My suffering has ended in this area, for which I am grateful, but will you please discuss it?

A: Take care how you listen to the voice of the flatterer, who, in return for his little stock of words, expects to gain considerable advantages from you. If one day you do not comply with his wishes, he charges you with two hundred defects, instead of perfections. (Saadi)

678. *Q*: It was a revelation to me to hear you describe true spirituality as nothing more nor less than a clear and undivided mind. Please repeat that idea.

A: Keep the imagination sane — that is one of the truest conditions of communion with heaven. (Hawthorne)

679. *Q*: We want peace with ourselves. Where do we start?

A: If we liberate our souls from our petty selves, wish no ill to others, and become clear as a crystal diamond reflecting the light of truth, what a radiant picture will appear in us mirroring things as they are, without the admixture of burning desires, without the distortion of erroneous illusion, without the agitation of clinging and unrest. (Buddhism)

680. *Q*: So self-transformation is the same thing as beginning to see things as they really are?

A: From all this it may be concluded that an unregenerate man is like one who sees phantoms at night . . . and afterwards, when he is being regenerated, he is like the same man seeing in the early dawn that the things he saw at night are delusions. (Swedenborg)

681. *Q*: It is our own insight that finally dissolves suffering?

    A: As sunlight scatters darkness. (Shankara)

Inspiring messages for you

a. Carefully explore the nature of pain and suffering.
b. Nothing satisfies man but to walk inwardly independent.
c. Surrender yourself to that which is truly right.
d. Spiritual understanding is your certain castle of safety.
e. Use anguish as a signal for turning to higher truths.
f. The self-liberated man cannot be hurt by other people.
g. Let unhappiness serve as lessons in psychic growth.
h. There is a way out!
i. Reject the artificial happiness in which most people live.
j. Let your inner guide lead you out of the wilderness.

10. How to Brighten Surrounding Conditions

682. *Q*: What is the fundamental rule for living peacefully and dynamically, regardless of what comes to us each day?

A: Make circumstances — all circumstances — conform to the law of your mind. Be always a king, and not they, and nothing shall hurt you. (Emerson)

683. *Q*: A detailed explanation of this would be helpful.

A: Fortune does us neither good nor hurt; she only presents us the matter, and the seed, which our soul, more powerfully than she, turns and applies as she best pleases; being the sole cause and sovereign mistress of her own happy or unhappy condition. (Montaigne)

684. *Q*: Is there a test by which we can know for sure that we are meeting life with cosmic rightness?

A: Touch what you wish with it, and it turns to gold. (Epictetus)

685. *Q*: In other words, self-change makes everything else all right?

A: The partial becomes whole, the crooked becomes straight, the empty becomes full, the worn out becomes new. (Lao-tse)

686. *Q*: Thousands of organizations around the globe are trying to make it a better world, but not much changes. Why is this?

A: There are thousands hacking at the branches of evil to one who is striking at the root. (Thoreau)

687. *Q*: Please comment on false human effort towards goodness and protection, that is, effort based on the illusion that wolves, masquerading as shepherds, care for and will guard the sheep.

A: The evil done by man falls upon his own head, without making any change in the system of the world. (Rousseau)

688. *Q*: I have never heard a truth which calls for a greater reverse in my thinking — a healthy reverse, I know. Because of this, will you please review the basic facts about man-made attempts to improve the world?

A: However much we have dulled ourselves with hypocrisy, and dulled ourselves with the self-suggestion resulting from hypocrisy, nothing can destroy the absolute certainty of that simple and clear truth that no exterior effort can provide us with security. (Tolstoy)

689. *Q*: Please explain how self-command provides freedom from exterior pressures and conflicts.

A: This external world is but the gross form of the internal, or subtle. The finer is always the cause, and the grosser the effect. So the external world is the effect, and the internal the cause. In the same way external forces are simply the grosser parts, of which the internal forces are the finer. One who has discovered and learned how to manipulate the internal forces will get the whole of nature under his control . . . He will be master of the whole of nature, internal and external. (Vivekananda)

The mystical meaning of victory

690. *Q*: We have been encouraged to think deeper and deeper about any idea which we think we already understand. There must be good reason for this.

A: Indeed it is well said, 'In every object there is inexhaustible meaning; the eye sees in it what the eye brings means of seeing.' (Carlyle)

691.   *Q*: What can awaken our dozing energies?

   A: Enthusiasm gives life to what is invisible. (Staël)

692.   *Q*: Please say more about inner liberty.

   A: Who is it that is to become free? You, I, we. Free from what? From everything that is not you, not I, not we. I, therefore, am the seed that is to be freed from all wrappings, and free from all confining shells. (Stirner)

693.   *Q*: Eastern wise men praise the power of non-action, which means to stop trying to force life to bend to our demands. It is certainly a sane course, but I need assurance that nothing is lost by this kind of active non-action.

   A: When we are doing nothing in particular, it is then that we are living through all our being . . . Will is suspended, but nature and time are always active, and if our life is no longer *our* work, the work goes on none the less. With us, without us, or in spite of us, our existence travels through its appointed phases. (Amiel)

694.   *Q*: Obviously, the mystic's definition of victory is different from that of most men. What does the mystic mean by triumph?

   A: My third maxim was to endeavour always to conquer myself rather than fortune, and change my desires rather than the order of the world . . . and thus render me contented. (Descartes)

695.   *Q*: Why must we do individual work to uplift ourselves? Can't an individual trust society for his rescue?

   A: And run to meet what he would most avoid? (Milton)

696.   *Q*: Will you please explain this idea?

   A: Society never advances. It recedes as fast on one side as it gains on the other. (Emerson)

697.   *Q*: But people are always planning new ways to

advance themselves and to be happy. If people never really uplift themselves with their activities, then what are they doing?

A: Doing nothing with a great deal of skill. (Cowper)

698.   *Q*: Is it correct to say that we need not strain to add anything to ourselves, but to live within our own natural and unpretentious self?

A: Simplicity, therefore . . . will contribute to happiness . . . Our existence will glide on peacefully like a stream which no waves or whirlpools disturb. (Schopenhauer)

699.   *Q*: It is obvious that human beings are doing something wrong, that we reject our jewels and wear the stones. What self-work can correct us?

A: It is the endeavour by the constant exercise of spiritual activity, to appropriate that infinite inheritance of which we are already in possession. (Caird)

How to win over all circumstances

700.   *Q*: In reflecting about these matters, I believe that the single greatest power we have is a sensible persistence towards self-awakening.

A: What sort of tree is there which will not, if neglected, grow crooked and unfruitful, but which will, if given right attention, prove to be productive, and bring its fruit to maturity? (Plutarch)

701.   *Q*: What might we add to our persistence in order to advance faster?

A: Method, like perseverance, wins in the long run. (Duclos)

702.   *Q*: May we have a method for maintaining peace of mind?

A: It is in your power, whenever you choose, to retire into yourself. Nowhere can you retire with more quietness or more freedom than within your own spirit . . . Constantly give yourself to this retreat, and renew yourself. Let your principles be brief and fundamental, and when you have returned to them, that will be enough to purify the spirit completely, and to send you back from all discontent. (Aurelius)

703. Q: Many people listen to and receive these ideas on the mental plane, but their lives still resemble robots.

   A: How can any external revelation help me unless it is verified by internal experience? (Eckhart)

704. Q: What is the nature of this internal experience?

   A: A new heart also will I give you, and a new spirit will I put within you. (New Testament)

705. Q: We speak of the need for *character,* but it is such a loosely defined term. What is the mystical definition?

   A: Character is the habit of action from the permanent vision of truth. It carries a superiority to all the accidents of life. It compels right relation to every other man — domesticates itself with strangers and enemies. (Emerson)

706. Q: This, then, is the foundation for pleasant feelings under all circumstances?

   A: It lies in our own power to attune the mind to cheerfulness. (Auerbach)

707. Q: I sense that nothing in the exterior has power to make us gloomy, but need more insight about our relationship to circumstances.

   A: We are *in* them, not *under* them. (Landor)

708. Q: What has carried us to the particular circumstances in which we find ourselves, and how can we change and elevate everything?

   A: Whatever we are now, is the result of our acts and thoughts in the past; and whatever we shall be in the future, will be the result of what we think and do now . . . When it comes, the higher powers and possibilities of the soul are quickened, spiritual life is awakened, growth is animated. (Vivekananda)

709. Q: Since self-change is the only road to changed and improved relations with others, what is a common but wrong attitude we can work to banish?

A: We are slow to believe that which if believed would hurt our feelings. (Ovid)

710. Q: What should be a man's major objective in studying his own mind?

A: To think from his own understanding, and to act from his own will. (Swedenborg)

You can refuse wrong influences

711. Q: What is the difference in the day of someone who lives with cosmic principles and someone who knows nothing about them?

A: Where one man shapes his life by precept and example, there are a thousand who have it shaped for them by impulse and by circumstances. (Lowell)

712. Q: You have urged us to distinguish between true morality and false goodness. May we have further aid?

A: Morality or the moral life may be described as that solution of the contradiction between man's higher and lower nature which is accomplished by the transformation of the lower into the organ or expression of the higher. (Caird)

713. Q: Each of us sees the world in a different way. Why?

A: Each heart is a world. You find all within yourself that you find without. The world that surrounds you is the magic glass of the world within you. (Lavater)

714. Q: Most of us insist upon doing things the hard way,

but maybe we can do otherwise when it comes to life as a whole. What is the simple and direct way to the new life?

A: There are some men — but the smaller number — who instantly, and as though by prophetic intuition, perceive the truth, surrender themselves to its influence, and live up to its precepts. Others — and they are the majority — are brought to the knowledge of the truth and the necessity for its adoption, by a long series of errors, by experience and suffering. (Tolstoy)

715. *Q*: Now that we know that all punishment is really self-punishment, how can we stop harming ourselves?

A: If you could see things as they are, not as they appear, you would no longer inflict injuries and pains on your own selves. (Buddhism)

716. *Q*: What is an effective method for remaining free of wrong influences?

A: Stand apart from circumstances, and do not permit them to influence the mind. (Zen)

717. *Q*: We are now aware of the false influence of the exterior world. What is right persuasion?

A: Let every man be fully persuaded in his own mind. (New Testament)

718. *Q*: What power can help us shut out the hysterical voices of the outer world, and think independently?

A: Nothing affects the heart like that which is purely from itself, and of its own nature. (Shaftesbury)

719. *Q*: What a victory would be ours if we were capable of being contented with what we have and with where we are.

A: If you are in Gyaros, do not let your mind dwell upon life at Rome; do not think about the pleasures offered to you when living in Rome, and all that would reward your return. Instead, be intent on discovering how the man who lives in Gyaros can live in Gyaros like an inspired man. And if you are in Rome, do not let your mind reflect upon life in Athens, but learn how to live in Rome. (Epictetus)

How to create pleasant circumstances

720. *Q*: I have been helped by realizing that we can go far beyond ourselves.

A: There is an immense ocean over which the mind can sail, upon which the vessel of thought has not yet been launched . . . Let us haul it over the belt of land, launch on the ocean, and sail outwards. There is much beyond all that has ever yet been imagined. (Jefferies)

721. *Q*: I have heard the teaching about artificiality being the enemy of freedom. Will you please explain it.

A: Horses and oxen have four feet. That is natural. Place a halter on the head of a horse, or a rope through the nose of an ox. This is unnatural. (Taoism)

722. *Q*: We would profit by understanding what it means to be natural.

A: He is great who is what he is from Nature, and who never reminds us of others. (Emerson)

723. *Q*: Where can I start to act in a different way, a way which creates pleasant and harmonious circumstances?

A: If you would do something, you must be something. (Goethe)

724. *Q*: Some human contacts look like trouble at first glance, yet we dazedly blunder in and out of them, often to our regret. What is wrong with us?

A: We are too careless and too self-absorbed to understand one another. Whoever has seen a masked ball where people dance together in friendliness, then separate and never see each other again, will have some idea of this world we live in. (Vauvenargues)

725. *Q*: What can we do when we feel far away from secure circumstances?

A: Exile is terrible to those who have, as it were, a limited habitation; but it is not terrible to those who look upon the whole globe as one city. (Cicero)

726. *Q*: How can I cease to get upset over daily difficulties?

A: You can remove out of the way many useless things which disturb you, for they lie entirely in your opinion towards them. (Aurelius)

727. *Q*: How does insight into other people kindle gentle feelings towards them?

A: If we could read the secret history of our enemies, we should find in each man's life sorrow and suffering enough to disarm all hostility. (Longfellow)

728. *Q*: I wish to confirm a certain point. As we make ourselves right on the inside, exterior improvements occur without effort on our part?

A: This simplicity expands itself little by little to outer things. (Fénelon)

729. *Q*: May we have a summary of both our actual life, and of the new life which comes when we invite it?

A: We are but shadows: we are not endowed with real life, and all that seems most real about us is but the thinnest substance of a dream — till the heart be touched. That touch creates us — then we begin to be — thereby we are beings of reality and inheritors of eternity. (Hawthorne)

Exterior events have no power over you

730. *Q*: There seems to be a much deeper meaning to these facts than the mind is able to grasp at first. Can a man's emotions, properly used, help to advance his understanding?

A: There is a deep significance concealed, connecting him, when he once has felt it, with the highest truths of the invisible world. (Robertson)

731. *Q*: The world seems like such a hostile place!

A: To a mind that is still, the whole universe surrenders. (Chuang-tse)

732. *Q*: I have the nervous feeling that people and events can disturb and shock me.

A: I saw that all things which occasioned me any anxiety or fear had in themselves nothing of good or evil, except in so far as the mind was moved by them. (Spinoza)

733. *Q*: What is a method for winning the self-control necessary for creating exterior betterment?

A: It is necessary to study the mind itself, mind studying mind. We know that there is the power of the mind called reflective. I am talking to you; at the same time I am standing aside, as it were, a second person, and knowing and hearing what I am talking. You work and think at the same time, another portion of your mind stands by and sees what you are talking. The powers of the mind should be concentrated and turned back upon itself, and as the darkest places reveal their secrets before the penetrating rays of the sun, so will this concentrated mind penetrate its own innermost secrets . . . It will all be revealed to us. (Vivekananda)

734. *Q*: The first higher truth I ever learned is still one of the most powerful and helpful forces in my day. It was the truth that self-liberty remains self-liberty, regardless of where the physical man may go.

A: Liberty is not in any form of government. It is in the heart of free man; he carries it with him everywhere. (Rousseau)

735. *Q*: So peace is not a place, but an inner condition!

A: In a village or in a forest, on land or sea, wherever venerable persons dwell, that place is delightful. (Buddhism)

736. *Q*: Is there a way to maintain peace of mind in spite of

exterior changes and disappointments?

A: Resign yourself to the sequence of things, forgetting the changes of life, and you shall enter into the pure, the divine, the One. (Taoism)

737. *Q*: Part of my mind still insists that exterior events can command my mind to think in a certain way, perhaps to think with pain. What true thought can work against this false thought?

A: It is in our power to have no opinion about a thing, and not to be disturbed in our soul, for things themselves have no natural power to form our judgments. (Aurelius)

738. *Q*: I want these teachings, but my circumstances are opposed to them, for example, most of my friends are absorbed by petty activities.

A: It matters little where a man may be at this moment; the point is whether he is growing. (MacDonald)

The greatest reward on earth

739. *Q*: The trouble with most of us is our endless demand for rewards — a greater reward, a vanity-pleasing reward, an exciting reward.

A: Reward? Do you seek any greater reward for being a good man than doing what is right and just? . . . Does it seem to you a small and worthless thing to be a good man, and therefore a happy man? (Epictetus)

740. *Q*: If people were to change inwardly, by receiving the truth, it would make a profound change in our exterior ways of life. What would happen to our ways of earning a living, to our relations with each other, to our medical and scientific programmes?

A: They would be different, richer, and higher, but would not at all be discontinued. What would be destroyed is whatever is false in them, while whatever is true in them would blossom and grow stronger. (Tolstoy)

741.   *Q*: How can we possibly change so many things?

A: Nothing need be changed but your hearts. (de Caussade)

742.   *Q*: I am like a man in a haunted house who has at least made his way to the windows to see the outside world. I know I can eventually break out.

A: In the meantime, of course, you must have patience. He who can see truly in the midst of general infatuation is like a man whose watch keeps good time, when all clocks in the town in which he lives are wrong. He alone knows the right time. (Schopenhauer)

743.   *Q*: Esotericism says that authentic power consists of inner qualities, like self-knowledge and self-command. How does it define false power?

A: All violence, all that is dreary and repels, is not power, but the absence of power. (Emerson)

744.   *Q*: Please say more about our ability to handle every kind of event with perfect poise.

A: The inner life is the only means whereby we may oppose a profitable resistance to circumstances. If the sailor did not carry with him his own temperature he could not go from the pole to the equator, and remain himself in spite of all. (Amiel)

745.   *Q*: Please show us what you mean by a heroic determination to achieve psychic success.

A: I have severed all ties because I seek deliverance. How is it possible for me to return to the world? He who seeks religious truth, which is the highest treasure of all, must leave behind all that can concern him or draw away his attention, and must be bent upon that one goal alone. He must free his soul from covetousness and lust, and also from the desire for power. (Buddha)

746.   *Q*: What a challenging but magnificent aim!

A: For the sake of this end there has been given to man the ability to elevate his understanding into the light in which the angels of heaven are, that he may see what he must will and must do. (Swedenborg)

747. *Q*: Is it accurate to say that true happiness occupies the same level as our clearness about cosmic matters?

A: As the mind is made intelligent, the capacity of the soul for pure enjoyment is proportionately increased. (Wallace)

Hear this magnificent message!

748. *Q*: These are the truths I have been searching for all my life. Now I need preliminary guidance.

A: If you want to be an astronomer you must go to the observatory, take a telescope, study the stars and planets, and then you will become an astronomer. Each science must have its own methods. I could preach you thousands of sermons but they would not make you religious, until you first practised the method. These are the truths of the sages of all countries, of all ages, men pure and unselfish, who had no motive but to do good to the world. They all declare that they have found some truth higher than that the senses can bring to us, and they challenge verification. They say to you, take up the method and practise honestly . . . So we must work faithfully, using the prescribed methods, and light will come. (Vivekananda)

749. *Q*: There must be a good reason why we are instructed to go beyond a mere collection of spiritual facts and plunge into a deep and personal experience with the truth.

A: A hundred thousand tongues may discourse to you about the sweetness of honey, but you can never have knowledge of it except by *taste*. (Caussin)

750. *Q*: If we really know ourselves, will we also know the right way to act in each human event?

A: If a man is a good judge of silver, he will know, for

the coin will tell its own story. (Epictetus)

751. *Q*: What should we know about ourselves in order to live with more rightness?

A: As long as a man stands in his own way, everything seems to be in his way, governments, society, and even the sun and moon and stars. (Thoreau)

752. *Q*: Sometimes I am tempted to climb towards public prominence, even though sensing its emptiness. What idea can help against foolish ambition?

A: I would rather go up the ladder to life. (Bunyan)

753. *Q*: I once experimented by putting more energy into a project than I thought I possessed, and was pleasantly surprised to see that the very use of energy increases it. This confirms our connection with limitless universal power.

A: He alone has energy who cannot be deprived of it. (Lavater)

754. *Q*: I am beginning to see why this way is the only way to genuine and lasting cheerfulness.

A: Heal your wounds, you wounded, and eat your fill, you hungry. Rest, you weary, and you who are thirsty quench your thirst. Look up to the light, you that sit in darkness; be full of good cheer, you that are forlorn. Trust in truth, you that love the truth, for the kingdom of righteousness is founded upon earth. The darkness of error is dispelled by the light of truth. We can see our way and take firm and certain steps. (Buddhism)

755. *Q*: You have said that our awakening consciousness enables us to hear a magnificently new message. What is this message?

A: There is another and a better world. (Kotzebue)

Helpful highlights of Chapter 10

a. You can have victory over all events and conditions.
b. Self-conquest is the key to exterior conquest.
c. Let these ideas become personal experiences.
d. You can learn to reject all harmful influences.
e. Take a voyage beyond your present mental states.
f. Use all your energies for self-emancipation.
g. Pursue the great reward of inner harmony.
h. Determine every day to win a new psychic success.
i. You can become a good judge of what is best for you.
j. The truth will make your new world appear.

11. How to Avoid Mistakes and Banish Obstacles

756. *Q:* In general, what is the chief obstacle to our discovery of the higher life?

A: Each has his own fancies, opposed to his true good. (Pascal)

757. *Q:* I have always felt inferior to other people. People who are famous or expert in even small ways make me feel worthless by comparison. This feeling now haunts me as I take up the task of self-discovery.

A: This is the meal equally set, this is the meat for natural hunger, it is for the wicked just the same as the righteous, I make appointment with all, I will not have a single person slighted or kept away. (Whitman)

758. *Q:* How can I conquer the harmful habit of giving importance to trivial and useless things? They drain all my strength and peace.

A: The man who lives in the true light and true love has the finest, noblest, and most worthwhile life that ever was or will be, therefore, it cannot but be loved and treasured above any other life. *(Theologia Germanica)*

759. *Q:* I am sure we are unaware of many of our obstacles. Will you please reveal one of them?

A: We cannot let our angels go. We do not see that they only go out that archangels may come in. We are idolators of the old. We do not believe in the richness of the soul, in its proper eternity and omnipresence. (Emerson)

760. *Q*: False information is that which a man picks up from others, from those who appear wise, but who stumble in the dark. Who is a man of true wisdom?

A: He is wise who is wise to himself. (Euripedes)

761. *Q*: Can you supply an example of what the mystics mean when they speak of an imbalanced man?

A: All other knowledge is hurtful to him who has not the science of honesty and good-nature. (Montaigne)

762. *Q*: We have just formed a study group with twenty members. Everyone has resolved to face whatever must be faced in order to break through the walls to freedom. May I carry back to the group a basic programme for success?

A: Only let your present and past distress make you feel and acknowledge this twofold great truth: first, that in and of yourself, you are nothing but darkness, vanity, and misery; secondly, that of yourself, you can no more help yourself to light and comfort, than you can create an angel. People at all times can seem to assent to these two truths, but then it is an assent that has no depth or reality, and so is of little or no use, but your condition has opened your heart for a deep and full conviction of these truths. Now give way, I beseech you, to this conviction, and hold these two truths, in the same degree of certainty as you know two and two to be four, and then you are with the prodigal come to yourself, and above half your work is done. (Law)

763. *Q*: I sense a unique richness in what you have said.

A: If any man has understood this sermon, it is good for him. (Eckhart)

Apply these principles right now

764. *Q*: I have no wish to continue with my old mistakes any longer, so my task is to make this higher level of living my own level. What is one way to succeed?

A: Truths, which enter with affection, are reproduced. (Swedenborg)

765. *Q*: Impatience has always been my chief foe. I am afraid it will hurt my task of self-development.

A: No great thing is created suddenly, any more than a bunch of grapes or a fig. If you tell me that you desire a fig, I answer you that there must be time. Let it first blossom, then bear fruit, then ripen. (Epictetus)

766. *Q*: Why do all the great teachers repeatedly warn people against false prophets and deceptive doctrines?

A: Many go out for wool, and come home shorn themselves. (Cervantes)

767. *Q*: I resisted it for a long time, but the mental dawn is beginning to break in one area. I now see why we are warned against those who love to publicly praise goodness and kindness.

A: It is difficult to persuade mankind that the love of virtue is the love of themselves. (Cicero)

768. *Q*: How can we learn to detect such hypocrisy?

A: Learn the value of a man's words and expressions and you know him. Each man has a measure of his own for everything; this he offers you inadvertently in his words. (Lavater)

769. *Q*: Why do we so easily accept shallow answers and foolish doctrines?

A: A mere trifle consoles us, for a mere trifle distresses us. (Pascal)

770. *Q*: In a discussion with friends, someone remarked about the uselessness of fighting against the truth. What statement would verify this?

A: For we can do nothing against the truth, but for the truth. (New Testament)

771. *Q*: If a man wishes to go through life with a practical and pleasant philosophy, where can he start?

A: The first business of the philosopher is to part with self-conceit. (Epictetus)

772. *Q*: Then a true philosopher is simply a natural person!

A: The less a man thinks or knows about his virtues the better we like him. (Emerson)

773. *Q*: We want peace with ourselves, but do not know what we must do.

A: The entire root of your problem is that you cannot get outside of yourself. (Fénelon)

774. *Q*: But in spite of all my working and reflecting and persisting I am still my own prisoner.

A: We are too fond of our own will; we want to be doing what we fancy mighty things: but the great point is to do small things, when called to them, in a right spirit. (Cecil)

How to make everything clear

775. *Q*: Maybe I have the wrong viewpoint towards my escape from psychic prison. Will you please explain how this might be so?

A: In fearing to make an effort to escape from conditions that are fatal to us, because the future is obscure and unknown, we are like passengers on a sinking ship, who crowd into the cabin and refuse to leave it, because they have not the courage to enter the boat that would carry them to the shore. (Tolstoy)

776. *Q*: Here again we find ourselves needing courage beyond ourselves.

A: Let not your heart be troubled. (Jesus)

777. *Q*: Because there is no real reason for feeling troubled?

A: The simple heart that freely asks in love, obtains. (Whittier)

778. *Q*: Please enlarge your explanation of obtainments.

A: A thousand illusions and follies are overcome . . . A thousand things become clear which were formerly enveloped in obscurity, and results are obtained which give a feeling of difficulties overcome. (Schopenhauer)

779. *Q*: You have stated that we harm others because we have first harmed ourselves. This is so important to see, I would like to hear it repeated in new words.

A: The soul of man does violence to itself, first of all. (Aurelius)

780. *Q*: I have been told I have a stubborn mind, which is probably true. What must I do in order to learn new and beneficial ideas?

A: Cease to cherish opinions. (Zen)

781. *Q*: By what method can we abolish false opinions?

A: Sell your cleverness and buy bewilderment; cleverness is mere opinion; bewilderment is intuition. (Rumi)

782. *Q*: We are urged to abandon our conditioned thinking, to return to the purity of our original minds. However, I cannot see anything wrong in pursuing the answers to life with the thoughts we have picked up by experience.

A: You know not, wandering one, where you are flying to. You will run into an enemy while fleeing from an enemy. (Gaultier)

783. *Q*: Your statement is confirmed by the individual and social chaos all around us. The cure is worse than the illness! We need a totally different viewpoint.

A: The new birth is here again the only power of entrance. (Law)

784. *Q*: How can we understand what is meant by the new birth?

A: Consciousness of error is, to a certain extent, a consciousness of understanding, and correction of error is the plainest proof of energy and mastery. (Landor)

785. Q: The first thing a man usually does when he gets into trouble is to look around for someone to blame. Please comment.

A: Regarding that which happens in harmony with nature, we ought to blame neither gods, for they do nothing wrong either voluntarily or involuntarily, nor men, for they do nothing wrong except unconsciously. Consequently, we should blame no one. (Aurelius)

The value of a new truth

786. Q: A chief neglect of ours seems to be the neglect of independent exploration.

A: We are foolish to depend upon the society of our fellow-men . . . they will not aid us . . . We should seek the truth without hesitation, and, if we refuse it, we show that we value the esteem of men more than the search for truth. (Pascal)

787. Q: Since carefully observing the secret motives of people, as the mystics have suggested we do, I am beginning to see how few people have really liberated themselves from themselves.

A: There are nine hundred and ninety-nine patrons of virtue to one virtuous man. (Thoreau)

788. Q: I am thankful for your exposure of the difference between shallow belief and practical purpose. Will you review it?

A: All belief that does not make us more happy, more free, more loving, more active, more calm, is, I fear, a mistaken and superstitious belief. (Lavater)

789. Q: I am afraid that I live more by sudden impulses than by natural wisdoms, for which I pay heavily. What is the superior way?

A: What your heart thinks great is great. The soul's emphasis is always right. (Emerson)

790. *Q*: The most baffling question to me is why we are unable to take advantage of the inner riches offered by God, Truth, Reality.

A: How can he grant you what you do not desire to receive? (Augustine)

791. *Q*: How do we become our own barrier?

A: There are few persons to whom the truth is not a form of insult. (Ségur)

792. *Q*: What information can make us want to toss out our touchiness and receive what we really need?

A: One great thought breathed into a man may regenerate him. (Channing)

793. *Q*: You say that artificial virtue consists in doing good in order to impress others, or to get a reward in return, and that people who do this always feel resentful. Please explain.

A: Virtuous people have almost always a slight suspicion of their situation. They think they are being duped in the great market of life. (Balzac)

794. *Q*: We have learned that no man consciously punishes himself, but does so only because he cannot see what he is doing to himself. What is the correction, for instance, whenever we react angrily to another person's actions?

A: Observe how much more pain is brought on by your anger and frustration over their actions, than by the actions themselves. (Aurelius)

795. *Q*: My present goal is to see the connection between a man's inward level of consciousness, and what happens to him in the outer world. What law operates here?

A: Each man reaps on his own farm. (Plautus)

796. *Q*: Personal experience has made me sceptical of what human beings call love. They call it love in order to conceal unloving motives. Is my analysis correct?

A: There are people who would never be in love if they had never heard of love. (La Rochefoucauld)

797. *Q*: Please discuss love which is worthy of the name.

A: Love is infallible; it has no errors, for all errors are the want of love. (Law)

How to avoid concealed traps

798. *Q*: Each member of our study class takes home the same idea for private examination and meditation. The results are then shared at the next meeting. May we have a good idea for next week?

A: Whoever you are, who read these lines, think about your position and your duties, not upon your position as landowner, merchant, judge, emperor, president, clergyman, priest, or soldier, which people temporarily call you, nor of the imaginary duties which these positions impose upon you, but think about your real and eternal condition as a human being. (Tolstoy)

799. *Q*: Am I correct in thinking that the purpose of this thought is to help us to value what is truly valuable?

A: What is a man advantaged if he gain the whole world and lose himself? (Jesus)

800. *Q*: Sometimes we pretend that we do not know how to help ourselves. What fact can shock us out of this excuse?

A: Every one of us, whatever our speculative opinions, knows better than he practises, and recognizes a better law than he obeys. (Froude)

801. *Q*: Describe a mind which has conquered many obstacles.

A: I call that mind free which jealously guards its

intellectual rights and powers, which calls no man master, which does not content itself with a passive or hereditary faith, which opens itself to light whencesoever it may come, which receives new truth as an angel from heaven, which, whilst consulting others, inquires still more of the oracle within itself, and uses instructions from abroad not to supersede, but to quicken and exalt, its own energies. (Channing)

802. Q: My question is about the matching of ourselves with the truth, which is obviously the only way to live accurately. To ask the question briefly, how can we *know*?

A: There is an inward state of the heart which makes truth credible the moment it is stated. It is credible to some men because of what they are. Love is credible to a loving heart; purity is credible to a pure mind; life is credible to a spirit in which life beats strongly — it is incredible to other men. (Robertson)

803. Q: Why do so many men find the truth about life too incredible to accept?

A: Every man's words, who speaks from that life, must sound vain to those who do not dwell in the same thought on their own part. (Emerson)

804. Q: I have the habit of walking dazedly into situations which later cause regret. I need a basic rule for seeing a trap before it catches me.

A: In every enterprise, consider where you will come out. (Syrus)

805. Q: Is it possible to develop this kind of intuition through mystical studies?

A: Principles are like seeds; they are little things which do much good, if the mind which receives them has the right attitudes. (Seneca)

806. Q: How would you describe our advancement through these studies?

A: A certain new light is communicated to the mind. (Baker)

It is right to seek help

807. *Q*: My personal obstacle is a reluctance to seek help and guidance along the mystic path. This is probably a combination of timidity and vanity.

A: All men who have sense and feeling are being continually helped; they are taught by every person they meet, and enriched by everything that falls in their way. The greatest is he who has been oftenest aided. Originality is the observing eye. (Ruskin)

808. *Q*: How can we escape being deceived by others?

A: Man is never deceived; he deceives himself. (Goethe)

809. *Q*: It is obvious that many public authorities appeal to human vanity and laziness, instead of teaching the need for self-facing and self-help. Why do such deceivers attract so many gullible followers?

A: There is a demand these days for men who can make wrong conduct appear right. (Terence)

810. *Q*: But it is still our own fault if we are led astray?

A: A man's own vanity is a swindler. (Balzac)

811. *Q*: Why do we hesitate to believe these damaging facts about ourselves?

A: Where belief is painful, we are slow to believe. (Ovid)

812. *Q*: What is an example of self-deception, of believing what we prefer to believe?

A: Were you to hear how your dear friends speak of you behind your back, you would never speak another word to them. (Schopenhauer)

813. *Q*: I do not understand how it is possible for a truth-seeker to maintain stability and cheerfulness. We are, after all, surrounded by personal and international suffering.

A: The greater the difficulty, the more glory in surmounting it. Skilful pilots gain their reputation from storms and tempests. (Epicurus)

814. *Q*: The habit of self-questioning has been praised by men who have found the way out for themselves. Please show us how a despairing man might phrase his self-inquiry.

A: But maybe I have overlooked something, or misunderstood certain ideas. It cannot be possible that this condition of despair is natural to man. (Tolstoy)

815. *Q*: Why do we so often miss the upward steps?

A: Why did you not look for the steps? (Bunyan)

816. *Q*: You have stated that esotericism reverses our thinking. I now see what you mean. Where we formerly sought praise and admiration, we now see through it.

A: In whatever way people may praise us, they never teach us anything new. (La Rochefoucauld)

817. *Q*: What obstacles in general must we overcome?

A: Delusions, errors, and lies are like huge, gaudy vessels, the timbers of which are faulty, and those who embark on them are asking to be shipwrecked. (Buddha)

How to make all events harmless

818. *Q*: You have urged us to observe these facts in our daily contacts with others, which I have done. I have a friend whose life centres around the collection of beautiful objects — paintings, furniture, flowers, and so on, yet she has no beauty of mind or spirit. This proves that the outer can add nothing to the inner.

A: Though we travel the world over to find the beautiful, we must carry it with us or we find it not. (Emerson)

819. *Q*: I have the bad habit of trying to force people and events to conform to my personal wishes, which usually backfires against me. What esoteric lesson can help me blend with events, instead of fighting them?

A: Leave all things to take their natural course, and do not interfere. (Lao-tse)

820. *Q*: I am aware of the need for honestly facing myself as I actually am, but find it more challenging than I first supposed. Is there something you can offer as aid?

A: It is therefore exceeding good and beneficial to us to discover this dark, disordered fire of our soul, because when rightly known and rightly dealt with, it can as well be the foundation of heaven. (Law)

821. *Q*: So is it good to see the bad?

A: The natural man in us flinches, but the better self submits. (Amiel)

822. *Q*: How might we more clearly see the necessity for following this new way?

A: Have the past struggles succeeded? (Whitman)

823. *Q*: Please show us how a faulty attitude leads to painful consequences.

A: I have tried to make friends by corporeal gifts, but have only made enemies. I never made friends but by spiritual gifts. (Blake)

824. *Q*: People use negative attitudes the same way they use weapons. We seem to think it necessary to battle our way forwards with all sorts of offensive weapons, like anger and pretence. Since they are harmful to both others and ourselves, why do they form a part of our nature?

A: None of these things should be called a man's, which do not belong to a man, as man. They are not required of a man, nor does man's nature promise them, nor are they the means of man's nature attaining its goal. (Aurelius)

825. *Q*: So part of our freedom consists in liberty from negative attitudes and emotions?

A: Don't be a cynic, and bewail and bemoan. Omit the negative propositions. Don't waste yourself in rejection, nor bark against the bad, but chant the beauty of the good. (Emerson)

826. *Q*: What is a major obstacle to self-contentment?

A: All the various ideas that arise making us believe that we require something external to make us happy are obstructions to that perfection. (Vivekananda)

The rules for a beautiful life

827. *Q*: Some of the Eastern teachings, like Zen, teach that obstacles exist only in our confused imagination. How would you say the same thing?

A: There is no one who hinders you from always doing and saying the things which are according to the nature of which you are a part. (Aurelius)

828. *Q*: What prevents us from acquiring these truths as personal possessions?

A: What we do not understand we do not possess. (Goethe)

829. *Q*: May we have an example of a self-punishing attitude towards spiritual matters?

A: Those who do not love the truth take as a pretext that it is disputed, and that a multitude deny it. And so their error arises only from the fact that they do not love either truth or charity. (Pascal)

830. *Q*: How can we detect that another person is really in the wrong, especially when he gives the surface appearance of rightness?

A: Few people are more often in the wrong than those who cannot bear to be wrong. (La Rochefoucauld)

831. *Q*: It is obvious that we must not permit negative people to stand in our path towards true life, still, we must continue to live in this confused world.

A: Let us live happily, then, free from all ailments among the ailing! Among men who are ailing, let us dwell free from ailments! (Buddhism)

832. *Q*: You have pointed out that we fall into trouble because of our inability to recognize trouble when we sight it. So consciousness must be the certain solution to all problems.

A: Every one who is in good can perceive evil; and he who is in truth can see falsity . . . Those whose under-standings are in light from wisdom are like men who at mid-day are standing upon a mountain and seeing clearly all that is below. (Swedenborg)

833. *Q*: If I understand correctly, everything in life operates according to intelligent and orderly laws, which we must discover.

A: The heavens themselves, the planets, and this centre, observe degree, priority, and place. (Shakespeare)

834. *Q*: So we can describe a right life as one which follows no rules outside of natural and beneficial rules?

A: Such is the picture of a beautiful life, and could we see it with our own eyes, as Plato says, great would be our desire to possess Wisdom. (Cicero)

835. *Q*: I would appreciate hearing a grand summary of our esoteric aim.

A: My cares and my inquiries are for decency and truth, and in this I am wholly occupied. (Horace)

Great truths for daily guidance

a. The chief obstacle to happiness is wrong thinking.
b. Become fully aware of faulty ideas and opinions.

c. Never accept shallow answers to life; seek deep truths.

d. Work faithfully on yourself, and never be discouraged.

e. Remember that you are seeking totally new viewpoints.

f. Love the truth, and have no desire for praise from men.

g. Refuse to be your own obstacle any longer!

h. These ideas enable you to avoid traps set by others.

i. You can remain untroubled in this troubled world.

j. Truth and decency should be our grand goal in life.

12. The Path to Easy and Natural Living

836. *Q:* What are the basic rules for winning a life of natural ease?

A: I am convinced, both by faith and experience, that to maintain one's self on this earth is not a hardship but a pastime, if we will live simply and wisely. (Thoreau)

837. *Q:* What is meant by living simply and wisely?

A: Every nature is contented with itself when it goes on its way well, and a rational nature goes on its way well, when in its thoughts it consents to nothing false . . . and when it is satisfied with everything that is assigned to it by the common nature. (Aurelius)

838. *Q:* My work as a salesman of office equipment gives me contact with dozens of executives and businessmen every week. I have noticed that one of their chief characteristics is nervousness. Could an executive living in these truths do his work with total ease and calmness?

A: His thought is quiet, his words and deeds are quiet, when he has won freedom by true knowledge. (Buddhism)

839. *Q:* I can see why inner freedom is everything. We must refuse to be captured by the surrounding social swindle, which passes for decency.

A: A horse which is harnessed to a wagon along with other horses is not free . . . The same situation is true of man. (Tolstoy)

840. *Q:* Tell us about the independent way.

A: Easy to walk by, inexhaustible! *(Bhagavad-Gita)*

841. *Q*: All of us get tired of battling and bluffing our way through life. We know we do things the hard way, yet know no other. How can we know this other way, this really triumphant way, of which you speak?

A: We need only obey. There is guidance for each of us, and by lowly listening we shall hear the right word. (Emerson)

842. *Q*: Then obedience to truth, to our original nature, makes the difference between a right and a wrong life?

A: Obedience ensures greatness, while disobedience leads to defeat. (Saadi)

843. *Q*: If I understand correctly, this obedience frees us of our own prison bars of egotism and self-righteousness?

A: Obedience is, indeed, founded on a kind of freedom, else it would become mere subjugation. (Ruskin)

844. *Q*: I am very fond of the principle that the truth is the most powerful force in the universe. Since it is helpful in a practical way, and also encouraging, will you please go into it?

A: Argument may be overcome by stronger argument, and force by greater force, but truth and force have no relation — nothing in common by which the one can act upon the other. They dwell apart, and will continue to do so. (Pascal)

845. *Q*: So this is what makes everything easy for a person living in truth, in spite of a violent world?

A: Here a man shall be free from the noise and from the hurryings of this life . . . men have met with angels here. (Bunyan)

A story from Ancient India

846. *Q:* How can I cure my anxiety over being separated from familiar things which give me a sense of security?

A: Diogenes was free. How so? Not because he was of free parentage, for that was not the case, but because he was himself a free man. He had cast aside every handle by which he might be enslaved . . . All things sat loosely upon him, all things were attached by slender ties. (Epictetus)

847. *Q:* What prevents us from living at ease with ourselves?

A: No man can, for any considerable time, wear one face to himself, and another to the multitude, without finally getting bewildered as to which is the true one. (Hawthorne)

848. *Q:* May I state my desire as simply as possible? I wish to be an entirely different kind of a person.

A: From this difference between the new and the old man, which is a difference as real as that between heaven and earth, several lessons of great instruction may be learned. (Law)

849. *Q:* What kind of real differences will we know?

A: If men knew what felicity dwells in the cottage of a godly man, how sound he sleeps, how quiet his rest, how composed his mind, how free from care, how easy his position . . . how joyful his heart, they would never admire the noises, the diseases, the throngs of passions, and the violence of unnatural appetites that fill the house of the luxurious and the heart of the ambitious. (Taylor)

850. *Q:* Then happiness has nothing whatever to do with public activities?

A: True happiness is of a retired nature, and an enemy to pomp and noise. (Addison)

851. *Q:* It appears that our mental health will match the degree with which we welcome higher principles.

A: Humility may be taken for granted as existing in every sane human being, but it may be that it most truly manifests itself today in the readiness with which we bow to new truths as they come from the scholars, the teachers, to whom the inspiration of the Almighty giveth understanding. (Holmes)

852. *Q*: Once we have heard and welcomed a new truth, what next?

A: Be like the pearl oyster. There is a pretty Indian fable to the effect that if it rains when the star *Svati* is in the ascendant, and a drop of rain falls into an oyster, that drop will become a pearl. The oysters know this, so they come to the surface when that star shines, and wait to catch the precious raindrop. When one falls into the shell, quickly the oyster closes it and dives down to the bottom of the sea, there to patiently develop the drop into the pearl. We should be like that. First hear, then understand, and then, leaving all distractions, shut our minds to outside influences, and devote ourselves to developing the truth within us. (Vivekananda)

853. *Q*: Please show us a difference between right and wrong self-work.

A: Our grand business is, not to *see* what lies dimly at a distance, but to *do* what lies clearly at hand. (Carlyle)

854. *Q*: I am impressed at the earnestness of certain people who have pursued these principles over the years. Most certainly there must be an attraction here which I must discover for myself!

A: Where there is honey, there are bees. (Plautus)

How to win the good life

855. *Q*: The mystics teach that happiness comes to us of itself, effortlessly, as we make ourselves inwardly right. Will you please explain what brings about this easy kind of contentment?

A: The sovereign good of man is a mind that subjects

all things to itself, and is itself subject to nothing. Such a man's pleasures are modest and reserved, and it may be a question whether he goes to heaven or heaven comes to him. (Seneca)

856. *Q*: In simple language, please tell us how to attain the good life.

A: Truth is the source of every good thing in heaven and on earth. He who expects to be blessed and fortunate in this world should be a partaker of truth. (Plato)

857. *Q*: But how can we determine what is truly good, when there are hundreds of contradictory opinions? What is considered a good act in one country is an unlawful act in another.

A: The answer to the last appeal of what is right lies within a man's own heart. Trust yourself. (Aristotle)

858. *Q*: Placing my confidence in exterior guides has brought me nothing but grief, so self-trust must be the only way out.

A: How easy it is to repel and to clear away every impression which is troublesome or unsuitable, and immediately to be in all tranquillity. (Aurelius)

859. *Q*: All this brightness and happiness can surround us even while we carry on with our daily duties in this frantic world?

A: The world is overcome, yes, even here! *(Bhagavad-Gita)*

860. *Q*: The mystics warn us against practising false goodness. What is an example of this?

A: We easily pardon in our friends those faults which do not affect our own interests. (La Rochefoucauld)

861. *Q*: You have made us aware of false security, such as dependence upon human authority, but will you explain

spiritual security? For example, is it possible to find steadfast restfulness in self-knowledge?

A: That which I know immediately and intuitively transcends in certitude all other knowledge, for the certainty of it is bound up with the mind's certainty of itself. I can no more doubt what I thus know than I can doubt my own existence. (Caird)

862. *Q*: Please recommend a way to make our daily activities as efficient and as easy as possible.

A: Beware of dissipating your powers; strive constantly to concentrate them. (Goethe)

863. *Q*: I recently read that most people are unaware of how they waste their energies by indulging in useless and endless talking. Please comment.

A: The first virtue is to restrain the tongue. He approaches nearest to the gods who knows how to be silent, even though he is in the right. (Cato)

864. *Q*: What an interesting idea! Up to now I had never thought of silence as a method for learning.

A: Study to be quiet. (New Testament)

True strength is effortless

865. *Q*: The mystics teach that the Higher Power causes all events to happen. Since this is so, how can we fall into harmony with natural events?

A: We ought not to lead events, but to follow them. (Epictetus)

866. *Q*: I sense something magnificent about the blending of ourselves with events. It must certainly end all conflict.

A: At this elevation, there is no effort, no struggle. (Suso)

867. *Q*: Do you mean that true strength, the strength arising from self-unity, is effortless?

A: It is as easy for the strong man to be strong, as it is for the weak man to be weak. (Emerson)

868. *Q*: If I could just get it deeply enough into my mind that I am both the cause and the cure of my own conditions, I would be inspired to elevate my inner state. Do you have a statement for making me feel this fact more strongly?

A: We make for ourselves, in truth, our own spiritual world, our own monsters, chimeras, angels — we make objective what ferments in us . . . We reward ourselves and punish ourselves without knowing it, so that all appears to change when we change. (Amiel)

869. *Q*: I have given myself the task of learning everything possible about a particular human condition, for example, I now see that an angry person is a frightened person. May I have a new condition for investigation?

A: The freer you feel yourself in the presence of another, the more free is he. (Lavater)

870. *Q*: One of the most helpful thoughts I ever heard was that the truth never needs to defend itself. I now see that our immersion in truth makes anxious self-defence completely unnecessary.

A: Truth is as impossible to be soiled by any outward touch as the sunbeam. (Milton)

871. *Q*: I often feel that I owe something for my bad behaviour in past years, but you say this is false guilt.

A: Come, there is no more tribute to be paid. Our kingdom is stronger than it was at that time. (Shakespeare)

872. *Q*: What prevents so many people from receiving the needed information about the easy way?

A: To speak and to offend, with some people, are but one and the same thing. (La Bruyère)

873. *Q*: We are told we have the ability to see beyond ourselves, for instance, we can perceive the cause and cure of

compulsive habits. How does this come about?

A: Just as by the telescope and the microscope we can increase the scope of our vision, and make higher or lower vibrations cognizable to us, similarly, every man can bring himself to the state of vibration belonging to the next plane, thus enabling himself to see what is going on there. (Vivekananda)

874. *Q*: And what *is* going on?

A: It is the Way of Heaven not to strive, and yet it knows how to overcome; not to speak, and yet it knows how to win a response. (Lao-tse)

A fascinating fact about happiness

875. *Q*: Please remind us of a basic principle, which we may have neglected, but which calls for renewed study.

A: The notion of cause is deeply rooted in every human mind. It is a universal idea, for all men have it. It is a necessary idea, for we cannot help having it, even if we deny its existence. It probably arises first in the mind on the occasion of our making an effort and seeing some result follow. (Clarke)

876. *Q*: How can we cease to produce negative causes and replace them with positive causes?

A: All that is required to produce it is simply the consciousness of what is in any measure greater than ourselves — the consciousness at each stage of our progress, that *something* lies beyond us. (Caird)

877. *Q*: Am I correct in seeing our task as ridding ourselves of blockage and contradiction, after which natural harmony and happiness flow by themselves?

A: Pleasure is the reflex of unimpeded energy. (Hamilton)

878. *Q*: It is fascinating to hear happiness described as the

uninterrupted flow of self-energy. Will you add a bit to the idea?

A: He is free who lives as he wishes to live. He is the man who cannot suffer injury, who cannot be hindered or compelled, whose impulses are not blocked, whose desires attain their purpose, who does not fall into whatever he wishes to avoid . . . So, no wicked man lives like this, and so he is not free. (Epictetus)

879. *Q*: Please supply a first step towards personal newness.

A: Man's life begins only with the appearance of rational consciousness. (Tolstoy)

880. *Q*: An acquaintance of mine remarked that he saw no need to work on himself when things were going smoothly. What is your reaction to this statement?

A: It is wretched business to be digging a well just as thirst is conquering you. (Plautus)

881. *Q*: You often remark that man has everything exactly backwards from the way it is in reality. Will you reveal one such area needing our correction?

A: Man does not wish . . . to come out of spiritual servitude into spiritual liberty, for the reason, first, that he does not know what spiritual servitude is and what spiritual liberty is; he does not possess the truths that teach this; and without truths, spiritual servitude is believed to be freedom, and spiritual freedom to be servitude. (Swedenborg)

882. *Q*: What knowledge can lift the servitude of being led astray by others?

A: A man often fancies that he guides himself, when he is actually guided by other people, and while his mind aims at one objective, his heart insensibly draws him towards another. (La Rochefoucauld)

883. *Q*: More and more I am seeing the necessity for choosing in favour of what is truly right for me.

A: The strongest principle of growth lies in human choice. (Eliot)

The great message for all!

884. *Q*: Please suggest a general method of self-work which we can use at any time.

A: Look within. Let neither the special quality of anything, nor its value, escape you. (Aurelius)

885. *Q*: So much that we do has no meaning, and the sensing of this emptiness is frightening. If we open ourselves to rightness, will we know what we are doing with ourselves?

A: The world means something to the capable. (Goethe)

886. *Q*: What prevents our inner nature from expressing itself with originality and spontaneity?

A: We are full of mechanical actions. (Emerson)

887. *Q*: One time in my life I became aware of the emptiness of flowery speeches and mechanical rituals. That is what turned me towards mystical studies. I want to get to the point of life.

A: Only show that you know how to never be disappointed in your desire, and how to never fall into that which you would avoid. Let other people labour at debates and difficulties and arguments. (Epictetus)

888. *Q*: Please describe esoteric self-confidence.

A: Virtue is bold, and goodness never fearful. (Shakespeare)

889. *Q*: I have read that the value of a principle is equal to the energy it takes to understand it. Please explain.

A: That which we acquire with the most difficulty we retain the longest; as those who have earned a fortune are usually more careful of it than those who have inherited one. (Colton)

890. Q: I feel that these ideas sometimes fall on rocky ground within me, which I do not want to happen. How can I prepare myself for them?

A: Men must love the truth before they thoroughly believe it. (South)

891. Q: That is what I want — a stronger fondness for what is right. Will my over-all studies develop this?

A: There is not only comfort and the ease of a burden brought to us by the sight and consideration of these, but an endeared affection. (Bunyan)

892. Q: We are told to examine exciting thoughts, and to not accept them as necessarily accurate. Why?

A: Because by so doing we incur the danger of being seduced, by mistaking our own imagination or perhaps natural inclination for the divine light. (Baker)

893. Q: Some friends and I have been studying a particular idea, stressed by Emerson, which is the enmity of society to individual freedom. Please add to our knowledge.

A: Culture, far from giving us freedom, only develops as it advances, new necessities; the fetters of the physical close more tightly around us, so that the fear of loss quenches even the ardent impulse towards improvement, and the maxims of passive obedience are held to be the highest wisdom of life. (Schiller)

894. Q: What message do such slaves need?

A: Tell them they are men! (Gray)

How to make life easy for yourself

895. Q: Please supply an example of how we unconsciouly make life hard for ourselves.

A: We are upset at being deceived by our enemies, and betrayed by our friends, and yet we are often content to be deceived by ourselves. (La Rochefoucauld)

896.   *Q*: What reply can we make when tempted to behave against our true interests?

   A: No, you can't deceive me. (Plautus)

897.   *Q*: The mystics say we should never hesitate to give ourselves surprises and shocks, for they aid in self-awakening. What kind of a self-question can make us think twice?

   A: Why should we be in such desperate haste to succeed, and in such desperate enterprises? (Thoreau)

898.   *Q*: Am I correct in concluding that self-study, while at first challenging, turns out to be the easy road after all?

   A: When, by analysing his own mind, man comes face to face, as it were, with something which is never destroyed, something which is, by its own nature, eternally pure and perfect, he will no more be miserable, no more unhappy. All misery comes from fear, from unsatisfied desire . . . When he knows that he is perfect, he will have no more vain desires, and both these causes being absent, there will be no more misery — there will be perfect bliss, even while in this body. (Vivekananda)

899.   *Q*: How can we invite this naturalness into our hours?

   A: Our individual life is but a phantom; make clear your eyes and see Reality. (Sufism)

900.   *Q*: We work frantically to achieve goals which we think will make us happier, and not only is the labour agonizing, but we are tense over results. If we become inwardly real, do our necessary daily duties become easy?

   A: All natural results are spontaneous. The diamond sparkles without effort, and the flowers open impulsively beneath the summer rain. And true religion is a spontaneous thing — as natural as it is to weep, to love, or to rejoice. (Chapin)

901.   *Q*: The best lesson I have learned in the last few days is the folly of seeking fulfilment in mere activity.

A: As soon seek roses in December. (Byron)

902. *Q*: Our study group is collecting basic facts about the higher life. My task is to gather truths of an encouraging nature. May I have one?

A: It is in men as in soils where sometimes there is a vein of gold which the owner knows not of. (Swift)

903. *Q*: If we uncover this spiritual gold, what changes will it make in the way we live?

A: Afoot and light-hearted I take to the open road. Healthy, free, the world before me ... leading wherever I choose. (Whitman)

904. *Q*: You are saying that as we find ourselves we also find our lives agreeable and easy?

A: Give me health and a day, and I will make ridiculous the pomp of emperors. (Emerson)

The easy way is the right way

905. *Q*: Please repeat a major truth which we need to practise with more diligence.

A: 'Know thyself' is one of the most useful and comprehensive precepts in the whole moral system, and it is well known in how great a veneration this maxim was held by the ancients. (Mason)

906. *Q*: What knowledge about our minds would help?

A: As rain breaks through an ill-thatched house, passion will break through an unreflecting mind. As rain does not break through a well-thatched house, passion will not break through a well-reflecting mind. (Buddhism)

907. *Q*: What does it mean to have a rightly functioning mind?

A: The mind is never right but when it is at peace within itself: the spirit is in heaven even while it is in the

flesh, if it be emptied of its imperfections, and taken up with
divine thoughts and contemplation. (Seneca)

908.   *Q*: Is it true that we possess an inner warning system
that signals us when we act unnaturally and with self-
damage?

     A: We are sure to judge wrong if we do not feel right.
(Hazlitt)

909.   *Q*: It was a revelation to me to be told that we cannot
try to be natural, but that naturalness happens all by itself
when we drop all efforts. How would you say the same
thing?

     A: Nothing so much prevents our being natural as the
desire of appearing so. (La Rochefoucauld)

910.   *Q*: I have been helped by your advice to not tie myself
to either the past or the future. May I have further comment
on it?

     A: The present alone is true and actual; it is the only
time which possesses full reality, and our existence lies in it
exclusively. Therefore we should always be glad of it, and
give it the welcome it deserves, and enjoy every hour.
(Schopenhauer)

911.   *Q*: Will our understanding of this principle provide the
quiet contentment we seek?

     A: On every mountain height is rest. (Goethe)

912.   *Q*: I have heard that an accepted truth multiplies itself
naturally. Please explain.

     A: The right will produce more right and be its own
reward — in the end a reward altogether infinite, for God will
meet it with what is deeper than all right, namely, perfect
love. (MacDonald)

913.   *Q*: How can a person begin to see that the easy way is
the right way?

A: He can already rely on the laws of gravity, that every stone will fall where it is due; the good globe is faithful, and carries us securely through the celestial spaces . . . we need not interfere to help it on: and he will learn one day the mild lesson they teach, that our own orbit is all our task, and we need not assist the administration of the universe. (Emerson)

914.   *Q*: You say it is our anxious clinging to our false ideas about ourselves that keeps us unnaturally tense, but what can we do?

A: Let go! (Hinduism)

Lessons about easiness in review

a. By living simply and wisely, we also live easily.
b. To drop pretence is also to drop strain and anxiety.
c. Mental health is the same as spiritual understanding.
d. Nothing is more attractive than self-transforming truth.
e. Discover the secret power of inner quietness.
f. Genuine strength is easy, natural, gentle, effortless.
g. Self-defence is unnecessary to the self-unified man.
h. Always choose in favour of your true interests.
i. Love the life-liberating truth, and you will have it.
j. Let go!

13. Solve These Mysteries and Enrich Yourself

915. *Q:* There must be some magnificent secrets hidden from us because of our own mental fog. How can we break into the sunlight?

A: There is no trifling with nature; it is always true, dignified, and just; it is always in the right, and the faults and errors belong to us. Nature defies incompetence, but reveals its secrets to the competent, the truthful, and the pure. (Goethe)

916. *Q:* If we could convince ourselves that self-delusion and self-punishment are the same thing, we would have a powerful force for waking up. Is that an accurate way of stating it?

A: Who is more deluded than he who is careless of his own welfare? (Shankara)

917. *Q:* I have seen a definite change and uplifting of my mind since going into these higher principles. More and more they seem to be the only things that really count. Do others experience this?

A: Those that are inexperienced may, and often do, call this a state of idleness and unprofitable cessation, as Martha complained against her sister, Mary; but those that have attained to a taste of it know it to be the *business of all businesses.* (Baker)

918. *Q:* Why do the mystic masters caution us against superficial belief, and urge us to get the facts?

A: Everyone believes in virtue, but who is virtuous? (Balzac)

919. *Q*: Can you give us something which will explain and reduce our fears of exploring the unknown? This is my major roadblock.

A: Our life is like a journey in which, as we advance, the landscape takes a different view from that which is presented at first, and changes again, as we come nearer. This is just what happens, especially with our desires. We often find something else, no, something better than what we were looking for . . . Instead of finding, as we expected, pleasure, happiness, joy, we get experience, insight, knowledge — a real and permanent blessing, instead of a disappearing and illusory one. In their search for gold, the alchemists discovered other things — gunpowder, china, medicines, the laws of nature. There is a sense in which we are all alchemists. (Schopenhauer)

920. *Q*: But doesn't this discovery require great inner power?

A: Do the thing and you shall have the power; but they who do not do the thing have not the power. (Emerson)

921. *Q*: You have rightly stated that most men and women are quickly offended by the slightest thwarting of their desires. Does the entrance of these principles give us a more mature mind?

A: Great peace have they which love thy law; and nothing shall offend them. (Old Testament)

922. *Q*: I have completed a work project which you suggested, with interesting results. You advised me to see that I knew almost nothing about certain ideas of psychology on which I prided myself. I now see that many of us are like a hobo who discusses the stock market.

A: A man is not educated because he talks much; the learned man is he who is patient, free from hatred and fear. (Buddhism)

Mystic principles are understandable

923. Q: How can we recognize true spiritual principles when we see them?

A: The principles of this authentic religion are entirely natural to man, so that the instant they are communicated to him they are received as ideas long familiar and self-evident ... These principles are quite simple, understandable, and few in number. (Tolstoy)

924. Q: What is the explanation of all the cruelties and stupidities which often masquerade as religion?

A: If we subject everything to reason, our religion will have nothing mysterious or supernatural. If we violate the principles of reason, our religion will be absurd and ridiculous. (Pascal)

925. Q: I can now see how the realistic principles of mysticism lead to mental health.

A: The root of sanctity is sanity. A man must be healthy before he can be holy. We bathe first, and then perfume. (Swetchine)

926. Q: How do you explain the persecution of genuinely good men, like Jesus and Socrates and Eckhart?

A: However evil men may be, they dare not appear to be enemies of truth, so when they persecute it, they pretend to believe that it is error, or say it is capable of crimes. (La Rochefoucauld)

927. Q: What are the characteristics of a person who makes self-transformation the first order of business in his life?

A: He reads much; he is a great observer, and he looks quite through the deeds of men. (Shakespeare)

928. Q: How is an enlightened man unlike other people?

A: Earnest among the thoughtless, awake among the sleeping, the wise man progresses like a racer. (Buddhism)

929. *Q*: What will keep us actively racing forward?

A: Let us beware of sleeping. (Bunyan)

930. *Q*: As a man climbs higher in the spiritual castle, will he meet and know others at the same height?

A: All powerful souls have kindred with each other. (Coleridge)

931. *Q*: What makes a mystic master the spiritual power that he is? What special effort has he made, what unique victory has he won which is a signpost for us?

A: The true critic strives for a clear vision of things as they are . . . his effort is to get free from himself, so that he may in no way distort that which he wishes to understand or reproduce. His superiority to the common herd lies in this effort . . . He distrusts his own senses, he sifts his own impressions, by returning upon them from different sides and at different times, by comparing, moderating, shading, distinguishing, and so endeavouring to approach more and more nearly to the formula which represents the maximum of truth. (Amiel)

932. *Q*: Some people use idealistic ideas as a means of hiding from their everyday responsibilities. What advice do they need?

A: Be a philosopher, but amidst all your philosophy, be still a man. (Hume)

The truth about an esoteric school

933. *Q*: What is truth?

A: Truth is the agreement of the mind with itself. (Plotinus)

934. *Q*: In other words, truth is the absence of self-contradiction?

A: It is your own assent to yourself, and the constant voice of your own reason, and not of others, that should make you believe. (Pascal)

935.   Q: Suppose we were fortunate enough to find a school of esoteric philosophy. What would it be like? How would it differ from common organizations which profess to help people?

A: A philosopher's school is a hospital. You should feel discomfort, not pleasure, in it, for on entering, no one is well and whole. One has a disjointed shoulder, another a wound, a third suffers from a cut, and a fourth has a headache. Am I then to sit down and give you a treat of pretty words and empty sentiments, so you may applaud me and depart, with neither shoulder nor wound, cut nor headache, any better for your visit? (Epictetus)

936.   Q: Would it be correct to compare esoteric schooling with the school of our childhood, for example, by learning to spell short words we are qualified to work on longer ones?

A: Now understand me well — it is provided in the essence of things that from any fruition of success, no matter what, shall come forth something to make a greater struggle necessary . . . the road is before us! It is safe . . . I have tried it. (Whitman)

937.   Q: Since esoteric truths are available to all who really want them, why does mankind remain in its miserable state?

A: Great truths do not take hold of the hearts of the masses. (Chuang-tse)

938.   Q: What a strange situation! Man is shipwrecked on a desert island, and not only refuses to climb into the rescue ship sent for him, but throws stones at his rescuers.

A: We are accustomed to see men scorn what they do not understand, and snarl at the good and the beautiful because it lies beyond their sympathies. (Goethe)

939.   Q: Why is it so difficult to shake a man loose from his foolish notions? You would think he would gladly exchange his self-punishing illusions for reasonable reality.

A: It is useless to attempt to reason a man out of a thing he was never reasoned into. (Swift)

940. *Q*: You say that a person of strong self-will has no conscience, and is therefore a danger to himself and to others. Please explain.

A: Self-will is so ardent and active that it will break a world to pieces to make a stool to sit on. (Cecil)

941. *Q*: A friend of mine is aware of his self-blocking, but sees no way out.

A: There is one direction in which all space is open to him. He has faculties silently inviting him thither to endless exertion. He is like a ship in a river; he runs against obstructions on every side but one, on that side all obstruction is taken away and he sweeps serenely over a deepening channel into an infinite sea. (Emerson)

How gain comes through loss

942. *Q*: The men and women in my study group find it helpful to hear the same truth repeated in different ways, so may we have your explanation of why the average person feels nervous and unhappy?

A: Not satisfied with the needs of nature, he demands the unneccessary. (Schiller)

943. *Q*: Please expand that thought.

A: All the ills of mankind appear, according to Lao-tse, not from man's neglect of the necessary, but because he does what is unnecessary. If men would practise what Lao-tse calls non-action, they would be free not only of their personal difficulties, but also of those residing in every form of government. (Tolstoy)

944. *Q*: Does not goodness consist in obeying the laws of the land?

A: What narrow innocence it is for one to be good

only according to the law. (Seneca)

945.   Q: Please help us solve the mystery of mental freedom.

A: I call that mind free which is not passively framed by outward circumstances, which is not swept away by the torrent of events, which is not the creature of accidental impulse, but which bends events to its own improvement, and acts from an inward spring, from immutable principles which it has deliberately espoused. (Channing)

946.   Q: You teach that with the loss of false values we also lose fear. What does that mean?

A: The man with an empty purse can sing before the robber. (Juvenal)

947.   Q: Will you please explain what is meant by psychic deafness? What prevents us from receiving healthy words and impressions?

A: Talkative people listen to no one, for they are ever speaking. And the first evil surrounding those who do not know the meaning of silence is that they *hear nothing.* (Plutarch)

948.   Q: If you have some especially strong medicine, we are ready for the cure.

A: Have you again forgotten? Don't you know that a good man does nothing for the sake of appearances, only for the sake of what is right? (Epictetus)

949.   Q: What is the explanation of human cruelty?

A: Fear is the parent of cruelty. (Froude)

950.   Q: By what means can we recognize an authentic teaching?

A: It must give us an explanation of our opposition to God and to our own good. It must teach us the remedies for these infirmities, and the means of obtaining these remedies. (Pascal)

951. *Q*: I would like assistance in understanding what you mean by false happiness, plus a technique for avoiding it.

A: A political victory, a rise in rents, the recovery of your sick or the return of your absent friend, or some other favourable event raises your spirits, and you think good days are preparing for you. Do not believe it. Nothing can bring you peace but yourself. Nothing can bring you peace but the triumph of principles. (Emerson)

You can escape the human jungle

952. *Q*: It would help me to understand a peculiar feature about worldly success. Once we win a certain goal, like wealth or popularity, it loses its great charm, and we feel as empty as before. Why is this?

A: Ambition becomes displeasing once it is satisfied; there is a reaction. Our spirit endlessly aims towards some object, then falls back on itself, having nothing else on which to rest, and having reached the summit, it longs to descend. (Corneille)

953. *Q*: We can never hear enough about the need for using our own energies for our own progress towards happiness.

A: The only elevation of a human being consists in the exercise, growth, energy of the higher principles and powers of his soul. A bird may be shot upwards to the skies by a foreign force; but it rises, in the true sense of the word, only when it spreads its own wings and soars by its own living power. (Channing)

954. *Q*: What should be our attitude towards the childish enthusiasms of society, for example, the enthusiasms of one pressure group against another pressure group?

A: Reason shall prevail with me more than popular opinion. (Cicero)

955. *Q*: We are told to depend upon ourselves and at the same time are advised to depend only upon God, or cosmic powers. May we have an explanation?

A: These two things, contradictory as they may seem, must go together — manly dependence and manly independence, manly reliance and manly self-reliance. (Wordsworth)

956. *Q*: This will eventually become clear to us, will it not?

A: If we walk in the light. (New Testament)

957. *Q*: As a student of psychology, I would like to know why a hard-hearted person is always the most easily fooled by false promises of friendship and love?

A: The less tenderness a man has in his nature, the more he requires it from others. (Rahel)

958. *Q*: It appears that what human beings call love is merely the exchanging of mutual benefits or the hope of gaining personal rewards. Is that an accurate conclusion?

A: He alone knows what love is who loves without hope. (Schiller)

959. *Q*: I try to choose a better way for myself, I really make an effort to select truth over falsehood, rightness over wrongness, love over hate, but my choice has no power behind it. I guess you would say I have no will power whatsoever. So if I cannot even choose rightness and succeed in my choice, how can I ever rescue myself?

A: You have no freedom or power of will to assume any holy temper, or take hold of such degrees of goodness, as you have a mind to have ... But you have a true and full freedom of will and choice, either to leave and give up your helpless self to the operation of God on your soul ... This is the truth of the freedom of your will. (Law)

960. *Q*: Please summarize the philosophy of the person who has resolved to escape the human jungle.

A: I did not wish to live what was not life. (Thoreau)

How your new life becomes possible!

961. *Q*: You have made us aware of how we all ask questions based in illusion, for example, we ask whether this or that human method will stop wars. It is illusory because we answer the question and then start a new war. What right question can begin to wake us up?

   A: The question at stake is no common one. It is, 'Are we in our right sense or are we not?' (Epictetus)

962. *Q*: That is what we really want — to be sane, sensible, unpretentious men and woman. However, our own negative nature deceives us into thinking this to be impossible. Show us how to challenge this false counsel.

   A: This power demands of us what alone is certain and rational and possible . . . which is possible only in the truth, and, therefore, in the recognition of the truth revealed to us, and the profession of that truth. (Tolstoy)

963. *Q*: By personal experience I know that it is a thousand times easier to find a religious charlatan than to find a man who truly knows what life is all about. Why is it like this?

   A: It is natural for great minds — the true teachers of humanity — to care little about the constant company of others, just as little as the schoolmaster cares for joining in the frolic of the noisy crowd of boys which surrounds him. The mission of these great minds is to guide mankind over the sea of error to the harbour of truth, to draw men back from the dark abyss of barbarous crudeness into the light of culture and refinement. Men of superior intellect live in the world without really belonging to it . . . they let no one approach them who is not in some degree freed from the prevailing crudeness. (Schopenhauer)

964. *Q*: Will you please comment on the special kind of communication existing between an esoteric teacher and his pupil?

   A: He teaches who gives, and he learns who receives. There is no teaching until the pupil is brought into the same state or principle in which you are; a transfusion takes place; he is you and you are he; then is a teaching, and by no unfriendly chance or bad company can he ever quite lose the benefit. (Emerson)

965. *Q*: It seems that the more honest we get with ourselves, the more we are attracted to esoteric philosophy, which proves that like attracts like.

A: Philosophy is a modest profession; it is all reality and plain dealing. I dislike solemnity and pretence, with nothing but pride behind it. (Pliny)

966. *Q*: I would like an example of what you mean by self-damaging self-deception.

A: The usual excuse of those who hurt others is that they do it for their own good. (Vauvenargues)

967. *Q*: We seek so many things. What is an imperative goal?

A: I have sought to know myself. (Heraclitus)

968. *Q*: I finally see what you mean by courageously discarding the false as a means of finding the true. It is like a detective who willingly tosses out dozens of false clues in order to find one right clue. But what a right one!

A: When the heart weeps for what it has lost, the spirit laughs for what it has found. (Sufism)

The secret of unlimited energy

969. *Q*: Since the universe is unlimited energy, and we are one with the universe, we can never lose by letting go and giving of natural goodness. Is that a correct summary?

A: Suppose a neighbour should desire to light a candle at your fire, would it deprive your flame of light, because another profits by it? (Lloyd)

970. *Q*: I wish to think deeply about a certain idea. Is it true that we get into trouble with other people precisely

because we occupy the same troublesome psychic level that they do?

A: As your enemies and your friends, so are you. (Lavater)

971. *Q*: We are urged to go beyond ourselves. What is the result of this?

A: On this road, therefore, to abandon one's own way is to enter on the true way, or, to speak more correctly, to advance to the goal . . . for the spirit which has courageously resolved on passing, inwardly and outwardly, beyond the limits of its own nature, enters the limitless higher world. (Yepes)

972. *Q*: No matter what I do to achieve success, I am thrown back in defeat.

A: If you seek Truth, you will not seek to gain a victory by every possible means; and when you have found the Truth, you need not fear being defeated. (Epictetus)

973. *Q*: Since guidance is within, what inquiry can we make of ourselves when in doubt about some comtemplated action?

A: Is this the way to the Celestial City? (Bunyan)

974. *Q*: What is the difference between happiness and shallow pleasures?

A: Pleasure can be supported by illusion, while happiness rests upon truth. (Chamfort)

975. *Q*: Does this new intelligence we receive from esotericism transfer itself to our business and home duties, I mean, does a more skilful mind make a more skilful hand?

A: As physicians always have their instruments ready for cases which suddenly require their skill, so do you have principles ready for insight into both divine and human affairs, and for doing everything, even the smallest, with an awareness of the bond which unites the divine and the human. For you will not do anything well which pertains to man without also doing well in the divine, and vice versa. (Aurelius)

976. *Q:* What is the answer to human quarrels and disagreement?

A: Where God is, all agree. (Vaughan)

977. *Q:* Can esoteric wisdom brighten my future?

A: Step out of your cave; the world waits for you as a garden. (Nietzsche)

978. *Q:* May we have some general information about the various impulses and urges which cause us to act for good or bad?

A: The central secret is, therefore, to know that the various passions and feelings and emotions in the human heart are not wrong in themselves; only they have to be carefully controlled and given a higher and higher direction, until they attain the very highest condition of excellence. (Vivekananda)

979. *Q:* I have made up my mind to never give up following these esoteric guides, but what reminder can help a person who feels he has taken a wrong turn?

A: Gradual practice makes him perfect, through a long series of slips, blunders, and fresh starts. It is just the same as in other things you learn. (Schopenhauer)

The miracle of self-awakening

980. *Q:* We are surrounded by misfortune, so it is encouraging to hear you say that a man in possession of these truths possesses perfect protection.

A: He is like unto the lotus which grows in the water, yet not a drop of water adheres to its petals. (Buddha)

981. *Q:* Please explain what the New Testament and other

spiritual sources mean by the new birth, by inner conversion.

A: Conversion is no repairing of the old building; but it takes all down, and erects a new structure . . . Conversion is a deep work, a heart-work; it turns all upside down, and makes a man be in a new world. It goes throughout with men — throughout the mind, throughout the members, throughout the motions of the whole life. (Alleine)

982. *Q*: We are told of the existence of all kinds of surrounding wonders, which we often fail to see. What is one of them?

A: There are wonders in true affection. (Browne)

983. *Q*: I am impressed by the esoteric fact which says that comfort cannot be found by running away from sorrow, but sorrow can be dissolved by inner wisdom. This seems to be a major truth.

A: There is no consolation except in truth alone. (Pascal)

984. *Q*: So many people, both the successful and the defeated, are sunk by feelings of futility towards it all.

A: Never say any man is hopeless, because he only represents a character, a bundle of habits, and these can be checked by new and better ones. (Vivekananda)

985. *Q*: Is it true that the great mystic masters can discern a person's level of consciousness by only a glance or two?

A: Wise men read very sharply all of your private history in your look and gait and behaviour. (Emerson)

986. *Q*: When I first attended lectures on higher truths, I heard about the practice of positive doubt. The principal point was that a man *must* begin to doubt the rightness of his ways if he is ever to see the light. This connects with the idea that man is unaware of his psychic sleep. May we hear more about this helpful practice of honest doubt?

A: As a man in his sleep doubts the reality of his

nightmare and yearns to awaken and return to real life, so the average man of our day cannot, in the depths of his heart, believe the terrible condition in which he finds himself — and which is growing worse and worse — to be a reality. He yearns to attain to a higher reality, the consciousness of which is already within him . . . Our average man has but to make a conscious effort and ask himself, 'Is not all this an illusion?' in order to feel like an awakened sleeper, transported from a hypocritical and horrible nightmare-world into a living, peaceful, and joyous world of reality. (Tolstoy)

987. *Q*: What is a particular mental newness of those who have found their way out?

    A: There is nothing for which they are so thankful as for that cry, 'Awake, thou that sleepest.' (Ruskin)

988. *Q*: The great mystery to me is how I could have been asleep to all this for so many years. I can now see what finally happened — I simply refused to go along with my old and agonizing life any longer.

    A: After a while comes the Great Awakening. (Chuang-tse)

Let these answers work for you

a. Self-awakening is your great adventure in life.
b. With right effort, you can understand all these ideas.
c. As self-contradictions vanish, happiness appears.
d. Detect and eliminate unnecessary actions from your day.
e. Refuse artificial pleasures; seek true contentment.
f. These truths bring sanity, intelligence, decency.
g. You possess the unlimited energy of the universe.
h. Always seek to go beyond yourself.
i. You can remain untouched by society's confusion.
j. Enter the miracle of self-awakening.

14. You Can Start a New Life as a New Person

989. *Q*: It is obvious that only a totally new self can be free of the confusion and the loneliness that makes up most of our days. I am sure there must be a certain solution which calls for our earnest attention.

A: Give yourself more diligently to reflection; come to know yourself. (Epictetus)

990. *Q*: Since healing principles are available to all, why do so many remain unhealthy?

A: Take a thorn-bush and sprinkle it for a whole year with water — it will yield nothing but thorns. Take a date-tree, leave it without culture, and it will always produce dates. (Abd-el-Kader)

991. *Q*: Is this why the mystics call for a total transformation of our inner nature, instead of performing mechanical moralities for public show?

A: The new birth, as signifying only a change of moral behaviour, is not only thus false and absurd in itself, but is also exceeding prejudicial to true conversion, and saps the foundation of our redemption. (Law)

992. *Q*: I am curious about a particular mystical teaching. While praising good works towards others, it insists that self-work must come first. Why?

A: We can only give what we have. (Amiel)

993. *Q*: What is the best course of action whenever we are tempted to do or say something which is self-defeating?

A: The truth is always the strongest argument.
(Sophocles)

994. *Q*: I need such a truth whenever I feel tempted to slow
down my exploration of inner space.

A: As the soil, however rich it may be, cannot be
productive without culture, so the mind without cultivation
can never produce good fruit. (Seneca)

995. *Q*: It is evident how we must prove everything for
ourselves. May we have a technique we can prove in today's
activities?

A: Take away your opinion and there is taken away
the complaint, 'I have been harmed.' Take away the
complaint, 'I have been harmed,' and the harm is taken away.
(Aurelius)

996. *Q*: I have made a list of all the sensible reasons why I
should be free of others, why I should never trade my inner
integrity for foolish rewards, why I must live my own life.
What might I add to the list?

A: There is one thing that, more than any other,
throws people absolutely off their balance — the thought that
you are dependent upon them. This is sure to produce an
insolent and domineering manner towards you . . . they soon
come to fancy that they can take liberties with you, and so
they try to transgress the laws of politeness. This is why there
are so few people with whom you care to become more
intimate, and why you should avoid familiarity with shallow
people. (Schopenhauer)

Your invitation to the new life

997. *Q*: I am impressed by the simple decency of these
teachings. Surely, decency and honesty is the only way out.

A: To be wiser than other men is to be honester than
they; and strength of mind is only courage to see and speak
the truth. (Hazlitt)

998. *Q*: I was asked by someone to describe the essence of esotericism. He wanted to know how it differed from the mere religious oratory of those who do not really know. What might I have told him?

A: We speak of definite truth which you can know by experience. *(Theologia Germanica)*

999. *Q*: You have explained that most men possess only a mechanical form of goodness, which is not true goodness at all. What does this mean?

A: Most people are so constituted that they can only be virtuous in a certain routine; an irregular course of life demoralizes them. (Hawthorne)

1000. *Q*: How can we have more than this morality of personal convenience?

A: The key to every man is his thought. Sturdy and defying though he look, he has a helm which he obeys . . . He can only be reformed by showing him a new idea which commands his own. (Emerson)

1001. *Q*: Please give us a new and uplifting idea.

A: Whenever evil befalls us, we ought to ask ourselves, after the first suffering, how we can turn it into good. So shall we take occasion, from one bitter root, to raise perhaps many flowers. (Hunt)

1002. *Q*: By what means can we prove the existence of a life far superior to the one we now have?

A: A man should learn to detect and watch that gleam of light which flashes across his mind from within. (Emerson)

1003. *Q*: What should be a major purpose in watching our thoughts?

A: To unmask falsehood, and bring truth to light. (Shakespeare)

1004. *Q*: I am trying to think in a new way towards a chief error of mine, which is the habit of blaming others for my frustrations. I am aware of it, but need a plan for collecting and retaining corrective thoughts.

A: A man would do well to carry a pencil in his pocket, and write down the thoughts of the moment. Those that come unsought for are commonly the most valuable, and should be retained. (Bacon)

1005. *Q*: I would like to feel that I have something worthwhile to do with my life.

A: Every morning was a cheerful invitation to make my life of equal simplicity, and I may say innocence, with Nature herself . . . The morning, which is the most memorable season of the day, is the awakening hour . . . some part of us awakes which slumbers all the rest of the day and night. Little is to be expected of that day, if it can be called a day, to which we are not awakened by our Genius, but by the mechanical nudgings of some servitor, are not awakened by our own newly acquired force and aspirations from within . . . to a higher life. (Thoreau)

The truth is compassionate

1006. *Q*: Freedom from illusion, escape from the social madhouse, and spiritual liberty, are all key phrases in esoteric language. Will you please define the meaning of self-liberty?

A: Our liberty, wisely understood, is but a voluntary obedience to the universal laws of life. (Amiel)

1007. *Q*: How can we acquire the knowledge we need for transforming our lives?

A: Truth becomes known through special exercises. (Buddha)

1008. *Q*: What is a principal purpose of these exercises?

A: To know exactly our own nature. (Spinoza)

1009. *Q*: Please suggest a starting point.

A: False happiness is like false money; it passes for a time as well as the true, and serves some ordinary occasions; but when it is brought to the touch, we find the lightness and alloy, and feel the loss. (Pope)

1010. *Q*: What if these exercises prove to be too much for us at the start?

A: Practise yourself, for heaven's sake, in little things, and then proceed to greater. (Epictetus)

1011. *Q*: If these teachings can change our hidden irritability and resentment into open peacefulness and kindness, that alone is enough reason for using them!

A: A good disposition I far prefer to gold, for gold is the gift of fortune, while goodness of disposition is the gift of nature. I prefer much rather to be called good than fortunate. (Plautus)

1012. *Q*: In studying the messages of all the great teachers and philosophers, I notice how firmly they speak against human folly. Often they suddenly switch from speaking of salvation and love to denounce human hypocrisy. Will you discuss this?

A: This resting in ignorance is a monstrous thing, and they who pass their life in it must be made to feel its extravagance and stupidity, by having it shown to them, so that they may be confounded by the sight of their folly. (Pascal)

1013. *Q*: As we advance inwardly, no doubt we more and more see such seeming harshness for what it really is — compassion.

A: They that be whole need not a physician, but they that are sick. (Jesus)

1014. *Q*: I lead an active life, but underneath it all I sense a vague dissatisfaction. None of my activities seem to have any real meaning. Maybe I am trying to run away from myself. Does life have an authentic purpose? How is it discovered?

A: I knew not the light, and I thought there was no sure truth in life; but when I perceived that only light enables men to live, I sought to find the sources of the light . . . And when I reached this source of light I was dazzled with the splendour, and I found there full answers to my questions as to the purpose of the lives of myself and others. (Tolstoy)

1015. *Q*: How can we qualify ourselves for self-transformation?

A: This great, good light and comfort is inwardly revealed only to those who are . . . inwardly illuminated, and who know how to dwell inwardly with themselves. (Tauler)

Dare to cross the river!

1016. *Q*: As a first principle of self-work, I have determined to never protect a false position I discover in myself, but to let it be replaced by whatever is truly right.

A: Your setting out is good, for you have given credit to the truth. (Bunyan)

1017. *Q*: May we hear more about the need for abandoning our old and burdensome ideas? How would an enlightened man explain it?

A: He compares the world to a dry, scorched, and barren wilderness, and celestial happiness to a most delicious paradise, divided from this desert by a deep and tempestuous river, which must necessarily be passed by swimming. The securest way to pass over this river is by quitting one's clothes; but few there are that have the courage to expose themselves to the injuries of the weather for a while, and therefore adventure over . . . Some few others (such are religious persons) seeing this danger, take a good resolution to divest themselves of their clothes, and to make themselves lighter and nimbler by casting away all impediments. (Baker)

1018. *Q*: Please challenge our esoteric efforts!

A: Do you earnestly ponder and sincerely try to understand? (Kierkegaard)

1019. *Q*: How can we tell whether or not we are beginning to work in earnest on ourselves?

A: When a man tells you that you know nothing, and you are not angry at him, you may be sure that you have begun to work. (Epictetus)

1020. *Q*: After some intense self-investigation, I now see why we must remain on our own grounds, and not lend ourselves out to others.

A: He who builds upon another man's ground, loses his mortar and his stone. (Cahier)

1021. *Q*: May we hear of a spiritual practice for use when meeting trouble of any kind?

A: Be not overcome of evil, but overcome evil with good. (New Testament)

1022. *Q*: Please identify a specific evil or mistake.

A: Despair is the greatest of our errors. (Vauvenargues)

1023. *Q*: I am certainly in error with other people. I appear to be at ease with others, but underneath I feel that the smallest wrong word on my part will cause an explosion between us. I would like esotericism to work for me in this area.

A: That is no reason for despair. You need not fancy it is impossible to regulate your life in accordance with abstract ideas and maxims . . . the first thing to do is to understand the rule; the second thing is to learn the practice of it. The theory may be understood at once by an effort of reason, and yet the practice of it acquired only in the course of time. (Schopenhauer)

1024. *Q*: I am now aware of a major problem to overcome. Men and women secretly cherish their unhappiness; it provides a peculiar satisfaction to retreat into sorrow and complaint.

A: To live we must conquer incessantly; we must have

the courage to be happy. (Amiel)

How to maintain inner poise

1025. Q: The speaker at our last group meeting said that the answer to any problem is hidden in the problem itself. May we have an example of what he meant?

A: We are not ourselves. (Shakespeare)

1026. Q: If we were shockingly aware of how little of ourselves we actually possess, would that change things?

A: There is no thought in any mind, but it quickly tends to convert itself into a power, and organizes a huge instrumentality of means. (Emerson)

1027. Q: Please explain the values of a clear and alert mind.

A: All that a man does outwardly is but the expression and completion of his inward thought. To work effectually, he must think clearly; to act nobly, he must think nobly. Intellectual force is a principal element of the soul's life, and should be proposed by every man as the principal end of his being. (Channing)

1028. Q: We are timid towards new ideas because they threaten our comfortable misery. What a test! We must plunge into the storm if we are to come out on its other side.

A: Thinkers are as scarce as gold, but he whose thoughts embrace all his subject, and who pursues it uninterruptedly and without fear of consequences, is a diamond of enormous size. (Lavater)

1029. Q: How can we maintain inner correctness and not get carried away by the mad rush of the world we must face daily?

A: Be sincere with yourself. Whether men love or hate, admire or despise you, is of but little importance. Speak only what is true, do only what is right. (Rousseau)

1030. Q: Surely there must be something much higher than our petty desires and our chronic agitations.

A: Every great mind seeks to labour for eternity. All men are captivated by immediate advantage; great minds alone are excited by the prospect of distant good. (Schiller)

1031. Q: How can we become more gentle to others, especially to those who cause us grief?

A: It is only imperfection that complains of what is imperfect. The more perfect we are, the more gentle and quiet we become towards the defects of others. (Fénelon)

1032. Q: Since self-honesty is a first principle of mysticism, let me speak my mind. I am tired of having others tell me what to do, what to think, what to believe, and what to follow. I want to follow *myself*, but I need more information.

A: A simple and independent mind does not toil at the bidding of any prince. (Thoreau)

1033. Q: I used to wrongly think that to be good meant to do things we really did not want to do, but now I see it means to do what is truly right for us. With this in mind, how can we benefit ourselves with more healthy goodness?

A: Let no man think lightly of good, saying in his heart, 'It will not benefit me.' As by the falling of raindrops a jar of water is filled, so the wise man becomes full of good, even though he collects it little by little. (Buddha)

1034. Q: This changes our psychic weather from cloudy to clear?

A: There are divine things more beautiful than words can tell. (Whitman)

Here is the way back home

1035. Q: All of us are like the Prodigal Son, separated from our spiritual home, and bewildered about the way back. What makes us wander?

A: To sum up all in a word: Nothing has separated us from God but our own will, or rather our own will is our separation from God. All the disorder and corruption, and malady of our nature, lies in a certain fixedness of our own will, imagination, and desires, wherein we live to ourselves, are our own centre and circumference, act wholly from ourselves, according to our own will, imagination and desires. There is not the smallest degree of evil in us, but what arises from this selfishness, because we are thus all in all to ourselves. (Law)

1036. *Q*: It would be heaven on earth if we could harmonize our own will with what actually happens to us. Can it be done?

A: If a thing is difficult to be accomplished by you, do not think that it is impossible for man, but if anything is possible for men and conformable to his nature, think that this can be attained by yourself, too. (Aurelius)

1037. *Q*: What is the specific process for winning this harmony?

A: We must follow, not force Providence. (Shakespeare)

1038. *Q*: And this provides a totally new life in the here and now?

A: The true heaven is everywhere, even in the very place where you stand and go. (Boehme)

1039. *Q*: I do not understand why the mystics say that a favourable change in exterior circumstances has no corrective effect on a person's internal state.

A: The seed of the oak produces oaks, and is never converted by circumstances into a beech tree. (Lotze)

1040. *Q*: Since opening my mind to what is truly right and honest, I have noticed a special change in myself. Less and less do I need to publicly prove myself, as I used to do, and as many people need to do.

A: Secrecy is for the happy — misery, hopeless misery, needs no veil; under a thousand suns it dares act openly. (Schiller)

1041. *Q*: It would help me understand my past mistakes better if you would expand on this thought. Are you saying that every attempt of a man to prove himself only increases his self-doubt?

A: He destroys his health by the pains he takes to preserve it. (Virgil)

1042. *Q*: Looking around at the frantic world, it seems that very few human beings understand this fact.

A: People of passionate temperament never understand this . . . They can only be impressed by acts and effects, by noise and effort. They have no instinct of contemplation, no sense of the pure cause, the fixed source of all movement, the principle of all effect, the centre of all light, which does not need to spend itself in order to be sure of its own wealth, nor to throw itself into violent motion to be certain of its own power. (Amiel)

1043. *Q*: We are instructed to observe and dismiss wrong feelings. Please expose one of them which we may be unconsciously hiding.

A: The worst kind of shame is being ashamed of frugality or poverty. (Livy)

A great mystical truth

1044. *Q*: The trouble with everything we have tried in the past is that it simply does not work. In spite of both individual effort and social planning, we are still bewildered.

A: We must approach this matter in an entirely different manner. It is great and mystical; it is no common thing, nor is it given to every man. Wisdom alone is not enough; a man needs a certain degree of readiness. (Epictetus)

1045. *Q*: If we make ourselves ready, what might we see?

A: It is a secret which every intellectual man quickly learns, that beyond the energy of his possessed and conscious intellect he is capable of a new energy . . . by abandonment to the nature of things; that beside his privacy of power as an individual man, there is a great public power on which he can draw, by unlocking, at all risks, and suffering the ethereal tides to roll and circulate through him; then he is caught up into the life of the Universe. (Emerson)

1046. *Q*: What is a basic difference between a wise individual and an unaware person?

A: The wise man recognizes the idea of the Good within him. (Plotinus)

1047. *Q*: Up until a short time ago I had not appreciated these true teachers and teachings. How can I speed up my appreciation?

A: In proportion as our own mind is enlarged, we discover a greater number of men of originality. Commonplace people see no difference between one man and another. (Pascal)

1048. *Q*: My main difficulty in achieving a better life is lack of clear knowledge of the way. I have tried all sorts of systems, but end up just as confused as before. Are there definite steps which anyone can take to transform his life?

A: True, there are, by the direction of the Lawgiver, certain good and substantial steps, placed even through the very midst of this Slough . . . these steps are hardly seen . . . notwithstanding the steps be there; but the ground is good when they are once got in at the Gate. (Bunyan)

1049. *Q*: Please give us an advanced spiritual truth to think about.

A: The individual soul should seek for an intimate union with the soul of the universe. (Novalis)

1050. *Q*: Is it correct to say that a man in self-harmony is the same as a man in self-honesty? By honesty I mean the seeing of himself as being one with the whole of the universe, and not as a separate ego which must battle with other egos.

A: An honest heart possesses a kingdom. (Seneca)

1051. *Q*: I am trying to see the difference between human power and power residing in union with spiritual principles. I believe it is accurate to say that spiritual power has none of the public screaming and general insanity we see in the news.

A: Power rests in tranquillity. (Cecil)

1052. *Q*: If we could only feel the existence of something higher than us working for us!

A: I am by Nature made for my own good, not for my own evil. (Epictetus)

Take this heroic forward step

1053. *Q*: It is incredible how asleep I have been to my own self-splitting. How will self-healing make things different?

A: All who have conscience say whatever they say from the heart, and do whatever they do from the heart; for not having a divided mind they speak and act according to what they understand and believe to be true and good. (Swedenborg)

1054. *Q*: So we must refuse to compromise, we must choose genuine self-change over the mere appearance of goodness?

A: Men, attached by habit to the existing order, shrink from attempting to change it, therefore they agree to consider this doctrine as a mass of revelations and laws that may be accepted without making any change in one's life: whereas the doctrine . . . . is not a doctrine of rules for men to obey, but unfolds a new life-conception, meant as a guide for men who are now entering upon a new life, one entirely different from the past. (Tolstoy)

1055. Q: So we can happily conclude that nothing is more practical than to return to our true self!

A: There is nothing more useful to man than that which most agrees with his own nature. (Spinoza)

1056. Q: Please discuss inner refreshment.

A: I have given you the refreshing drink called the perception of truth, and he who drinks of it becomes free from excitement, passion, and wrong-doing. (Buddha)

1057. Q: A friend of mine is becoming more and more interested in higher truth, but has trouble understanding why his progress is so slow. What might I tell him?

A: When a farmer is irrigating his field the water is already in the canals, only there are gates which keep the water in. The farmer opens these gates, and the water flows in by itself, by the law of gravitation. So, all human progress and power are already in everything; this perfection is every man's nature, only it is barred in and prevented from taking its proper course. If anyone can take the bar off, in rushes nature. Then the man attains the powers which are his already. (Vivekananda)

1058. Q: Then our happiness depends upon how much we permit ourselves to be our real selves?

A: We make for ourselves, in truth, our own spiritual world. (Amiel)

1059. Q: Suppose a man reaches the point where he sees, at least dimly, the anger and the terror and the frustration he has concealed so long from himself and others. Suppose his suffering has also given him a glimpse of the light at the exit of his cave. What forward step can he take?

A: It is time to undervalue what he has valued, to dispossess himself of what he has acquired, and with Caesar to take in his hand the army, the empire and Cleopatra, and say, 'All these will I relinquish, if you will show me the fountains of the Nile.' (Emerson)

1060. *Q*: That is the heroism we all need.

A: I know that they go towards the best — towards something great. (Whitman)

Methods for changing your life

a. Anyone can become a totally new individual.
b. Self-transformation comes through esoteric self-work.
c. Life invites you to discover its true brightness!
d. The nature of truth is kindness and compassion.
e. Have the courage to be a new and a happy person.
f. Refuse to be carried away by exterior confusion.
g. Your new life is beautiful beyond all description.
h. Determine to return home to your true nature.
i. The truth always works, if we let it.
j. Something new and great is just ahead of you.

15. How to Swiftly Awaken Your Hidden Powers

1061. *Q*: Do I understand correctly that we actually possess all the strength we need, but have failed to draw from it?

A: Beast, birds, and insects, even to the minutest and meanest of their kind, act with the unerring providence of instinct; man, the while, who possesses a higher faculty, abuses it, and therefore goes blundering on. (Southey)

1062. *Q*: What is a common way in which people abuse their natural powers?

A: To pursue trifles is the lot of humanity; and whether we bustle in a pantomime or strut at a coronation, whether we shout at a bonfire or harangue in a senate-house — whatever object we follow, it will at last surely conduct us to futility and disappointment. (Goldsmith)

1063. *Q*: You seem to be saying that we beat upon a thousand exciting drums in a frantic attempt to drown out the noise of our own pains.

A: For my part, I would rather there were less of such excitement and transport, less of mere thrilling emotion, so that a man were diligent and rightly manful in working and in virtue, for in such exercises do we learn best to know ourselves. (Tauler)

1064. *Q*: What prevents people from making clear and realistic thinking a permanent power for self-guidance?

A: With a large number of people, it is quite evident that their power of sight wholly predominates over their power of thought; they seem to be conscious of their existence only when they are making a noise. (Schopenhauer)

1065. Q: I do not see how the restoration of our inner faculties connects with vital spiritual matters.

A: When everything is in its right place within us, we ourselves are in balance with the whole work of God. (Amiel)

1066. Q: Some people like the kind of power that tyrannizes and hurts other people. This is obviously false and evil power, based on deceitful appearances, and backed up by the lunatic mob. What is true power?

A: Power obeys reality, and not appearances; power is according to quality, and not quantity. (Emerson)

1067. Q: Sometimes we get so involved with our own thinking that we forget the simplest of rules for successful living. Please remind us of one.

A: We should not act and speak as if we were asleep. (Aurelius)

1068. Q: Esotericism teaches that men dwell in a peculiar state of spiritual sleep, while dreaming that they are awake. What information can begin to shake us awake?

A: Reality surpasses imagination, and we see breathing, brightening and moving before our eyes some sights dearer to our hearts than any we ever beheld in the land of sleep. (Goethe)

1069. Q: My husband and I would appreciate having an exercise we can work out together.

A: Every night we should call ourselves to account: 'What weakness have I overcome today? What passions opposed? What temptations resisted? What virtue acquired?' Our weaknesses will decrease of themselves if they are brought every day to the light. (Seneca)

How to awaken fresh energy

1070. Q: I feel more and more attracted to these ideas

because they have a certain charm and radiance found in no other place. Is my experience shared by others?

A: It is only through the morning gate of the beautiful that you can penetrate into the realm of knowledge. That which we feel here as beauty, we shall one day know as truth. (Schiller)

1071. *Q*: You have said that many of these ideas may seem negative at first, but turn out to be the very map to the treasure. Will you please cite an instance of this?

A: The precept, 'Know yourself' was not solely intended to abolish the pride of men, but also that we might understand our own value. (Cicero)

1072. *Q*: The talent for turning negative impulses into constructive forces seems like true magic to me. It would be valuable, for example, to turn a strong feeling of persecution into the feeling that there is truly another way to live.

A: Strong impulses are but another name for energy. Energy may be turned to bad uses, but more good may always be made of an energetic nature, than of an indolent and impassive one. (Mill)

1073. *Q*: Do I understand correctly that fresh energy develops as we actually engage in the battle for inner rightness?

A: Our energy is in proportion to the resistance we meet. (Hazlitt)

1074. *Q*: I am wondering if this is why self-reliance is so highly prized by those who have found their way out of the cave? I mean, if we cease to lean on others, we must lean on ourselves, which forces our slumbering energies to awaken.

A: A man is best off if he is thrown upon his own resources, and can be all in all to himself, and Cicero goes so far as to say that a man who is in this condition cannot fail to be very happy. (Schopenhauer)

1075. *Q*: Does self-dependence have a limit?

A: No bird soars too high, if he soars with his own wings. (Blake)

1076. *Q*: You say that our faithful study of these messages produces a change in our feeling towards them. By this I believe you mean that we value them more and therefore make them more and more welcome.

A: Welcome as kindly showers to the long parched earth. (Dryden)

1077. *Q*: How can we release our psychic forces in the shortest possible time?

A: The greatest loss of time is delay and expectation, which depends upon the future. We let go of the present, which we have in our power, and look forward to that which depends upon chance — and so relinquish a certainty for an uncertainty. (Seneca)

1078. *Q*: I am delighted at how my clear understanding of even one idea has power to solve a dozen problems. It is like having a single clear window, which is enough to see everything immediately outside.

A: A new principle is an inexhaustible source of new views. (Vauvenargues)

Your map for the esoteric journey

1079. *Q*: All of us realize the need for independent mental work, but it is so tempting to simply adopt the poisonous notions manufactured by the masses. Give an antidote for maintaining total mental health.

A: Prove all things; hold fast that which is good. (New Testament)

1080. *Q*: I need a simplified explanation of why we are working to see ourselves as we really are, instead of seeing ourselves through our vanities. What is the value in this disturbing of ourselves?

A: I am in the process of bringing all my defects into the light for the purpose of getting rid of them. We never know how rich we are until we break up housekeeping! (Hénault)

1081. *Q*: May we have general information about our hidden powers?

A: Although men are accused for not knowing their own weakness, yet perhaps as few know their strength. It is in men as in soils, where sometimes there is a vein of gold which the owner knows not of. (Swift)

1082. *Q*: And we will be aware of the actual rising of these new forces?

A: These you shall see. (Epictetus)

1083. *Q*: What power do we have over those discomforts we meet as we circulate among people and events?

A: If you are pained by any external thing, it is not this thing that disturbs you, but your own judgment about it. It is in your power to erase this judgment now. If anything in your own nature gives you pain, who hinders you from correcting your opinion? (Aurelius)

1084. *Q*: I have run out of excuses, so I must now take up these ideas as a major task in life. Please show me where I have failed to unite with my own powers for self-rescue.

A: We are never present with, but always beyond ourselves. Fear, desire, and hope are always pushing us towards the future. (Montaigne)

1085. *Q*: Is this why esotericism stresses the need for self-unity, for being one with ourselves?

A: Philosophy is, to tell the truth, a homesickness, an effort to return home. (Novalis)

1086. *Q*: Please provide a map for those who want to make the return trip.

A: The custom of frequent reflection will keep their minds from running adrift, and call their thoughts home from useless, inattentive roving. (Locke)

1087. *Q*: Insight into our desires is no doubt very valuable to us, but specifically, how can an understanding of our desires keep us out of trouble?

A: We would desire few things ardently if we had a perfect knowledge of what we were desiring. (La Rochefoucauld)

1088. *Q*: Our aim is to become real. What is your definition of a real person?

A: The most virtuous of all men is he who contents himself with being virtuous without seeking to appear so. (Plato)

Anyone can recover his natural powers

1089. *Q*: We are collecting a rich harvest of ideas for our mental storehouse. May we have a procedure for using them for maximum value?

A: We ought never to be afraid to repeat an ancient truth when we feel that we can make it more striking by a neater turn, or bring it alongside of another truth, which may make it clearer, and thereby accumulate evidence. It belongs to the inventive faculty to see clearly the relative state of things, and to be able to place them in connection, but the discoveries of past ages belong less to their first authors than to those who make them practically useful to the world. (Vauvenargues)

1090. *Q*: I would like assurance that nothing — absolutely nothing — can prevent a sincere man from recovering the original powers he lost by choosing fancy over fact.

A: A sublime soul can rise to all kinds of greatness, but by his own effort; it can tear itself loose from all bondage, to all that limits and restrains it, but only by the strength of determination. (Schiller)

1091. *Q*: It seems that right aspirations are important.

A: A good intention clothes itself with sudden power. (Emerson)

1092. *Q*: I am aware that we must make the venture towards the higher life, but half the time we are not sure of what we are doing.

A: If a man constantly aspires, is he not elevated? Did ever a man try heroism, magnanimity, truth, sincerity, and find that there was no advantage in them — that it was a vain endeavour? (Thoreau)

1093. *Q*: Our receptivity to truth is a cause which produces an effect. What is that effect?

A: The fruit of the Spirit is love, joy, peace. (New Testament)

1094. *Q*: We feel the painful consequences of our faults, yet are so reluctant to work at self-purification. At what point will we be able to admit more faults as a first step towards ending them?

A: Why does no man confess his vices? Because he is still in them. It is for a waking man to tell of his dreams. (Seneca)

1095. *Q*: You teach that our approach towards true life must be dynamically different from the methods used in everyday business. What is that difference?

A: Human things must be known to be loved, but Divine things must be loved to be known. (Pascal)

1096. *Q*: May I review? Esotericism teaches that our only real task in life is to awaken from our terrible psychic slumber, to become conscious and aware men and women. In this newness we have no more problems, because we have banished the cause of problems — our own unconsciousness, our unawareness.

A: Men must be aware of the wisdom and the strength

that is in them if their understanding is to be expanded. (Vauvenargues)

1097. *Q*: Awareness, consciousness, is everything?

A: Man finds joy in himself, and, safe in the inaccessible sanctuary of his personal consciousness, becomes almost a god. He is himself principle, motive, and the end of his own destiny; he is himself, and that is enough for him. (Amiel)

Look in an entirely new direction!

1098. *Q*: You are teaching us to look in an entirely new direction, which I know is the only right way. As an aid, please illustrate how we look in the wrong direction.

A: Suppose that, with the exception of some sore or painful spot, we are physically in a sound and healthy condition. The pain of this one spot will completely absorb our attention, causing us to lose the sense of general well-being, and destroying our comfort in life. In the same way, when all our affairs but one turn out as we wish, the single instance in which our aims are frustrated is a constant trouble to us, even though it is something quite trivial. (Schopenhauer)

1099. *Q*: How can this fault be corrected?

A: Today I have escaped from all trouble, or rather, I have cast out all trouble, for it was not outside me, but within, and in my opinions. (Aurelius)

1100. *Q*: Why do many public authorities have the facts about inner power, but show by their private lives that they lack the power itself?

A: The walls of rude minds are scrawled all over with facts, with thoughts. They shall one day bring a lantern and read the inscriptions. (Emerson)

1101. *Q*: Then a fact and an understanding of that fact are different things?

A: It is the understanding that sees and hears; it is the understanding that improves everything, that orders everything, and that acts, rules, and reigns. (Epicharmus)

1102. *Q*: What kind of person can receive these powers of understanding?

A: He that hath ears to hear, let him hear. (Jesus)

1103. *Q*: What new message might we hear from our awakened understanding?

A: What a brave privilege it is to be free from all contentions, from all envying or being envied, from receiving or paying all kinds of ceremonies! (Cowley)

1104. *Q*: I wonder whether we will ever really learn. We always follow human idols and we always pay the price.

A: The great are only great because we are on our knees. Let us rise up. (Proudhon)

1105. *Q*: Though it makes us uncomfortable at first, it seems like a good idea to remember what we are missing by not pursuing truth. May we have such a reminder?

A: The man who has no refuge in himself, who lives, so to speak, in his front rooms, in the outer whirlwind of things and opinions, is not properly speaking a personality at all; he is not distinct, free, original, a cause — in a word, *someone*. He is one of the crowd, a taxpayer, an elector, an anonymity, but not a man. (Amiel)

1106. *Q*: Why are we so careless of our spiritual prosperity?

A: Our indifference to the truth is due to our determination to follow our desires. 'It is of no importance,' men say, 'to know where the truth is, since we know what will give us pleasure.' (Vauvenargues)

Explore beyond your present boundaries

1107. *Q*: Man has been compared to a ship without a rudder, which every wind catches and drives back and forth, up and down. How can we take charge of our psychic ship, so that it is not at the mercy of another person's frown or of unwanted news?

A: Man is obviously made to think. It is his whole dignity and his whole merit and his whole duty to think as he ought. (Pascal)

1108. *Q*: How can we increase our mental powers?

A: Nothing has such power to broaden the mind as the ability to investigate systematically and truly all that comes under your observation in life. (Aurelius)

1109. *Q*: I would like to investigate the principle which proclaims man's ability to know both the cause and cure of his own disaster.

A: All things are known to the soul. It is not to be surprised by any communication. Nothing can be greater than it, let those fear and those fawn who will. The soul is in her native realm; and it is wider than space, older than time, wide as hope, rich as love. Pusillanimity and fear she refuses with a beautiful scorn; they are not for her who putteth on her coronation robes, and goes out through universal love to universal power. (Emerson)

1110. *Q*: Why do many people, including ourselves, hesitate to explore beyond our present boundaries of life?

A: Narrowness of mind is the cause of obstinacy — we do not easily believe what is beyond our sight. (La Rochefoucauld)

1111. *Q*: But why should people change their minds? It is supposed to be noble to stand by one's convictions.

A: Stubbornness is not firmness. (Schiller)

1112. *Q*: I realize the need for giving these wisdoms an opportunity to change me in a new way. How can I do so?

A: It is love that asks, that seeks, that knocks, that

finds, and that is faithful to what it finds. (Augustine)

1113. Q: Sometimes we feel that the only good things are those we can see or touch. What is the answer to this misleading temptation?

A: The true harvest of my daily life is somewhat as intangible and indescribable as the tints of morning or evening. It is a little star-dust caught, a segment of the rainbow which I have clutched. (Thoreau)

1114. Q: All of us sense that whatever is natural is always right and healthy, so please tell us how to recognize both the natural and the unnatural.

A: Where there is much pretence, much has been borrowed — nature never pretends. (Lavater)

1115. Q: I find it helpful to see our inner forces as servants which work for us silently and efficiently.

A: Untwisting all the chains that tie the hidden soul of harmony. (Milton)

Absorb these vital facts about life

1116. Q: Of the hundreds of interesting facts we have un-covered, one of the most surprising is man's immersion in illusions about his identity. He falsely thinks he has a sepa-rate self, with separate self-wisdom and self-control, instead of seeing that he lives in Cosmic Oneness, in Universal Mind. Please confirm this.

A: Nothing is more hidden from us than the illusion which lives with us day by day, and our greatest illusion is to believe that we are what we think ourselves to be. (Amiel)

1117. Q: What is meant by Universal Mind?

A: There is one mind common to all individual men. Every man is an inlet to the same and to all of the same. He that is once admitted to the right of reason is made a freeman of the whole estate. What Plato has thought, he may think;

what a saint has felt, he may feel; what at any time has befallen any man, he can understand. Who hath access to this universal mind is a party to all that is or can be done, for this is the only and sovereign agent. (Emerson)

1118. Q: Your teaching about the Oneness of man with his universe is both practical and fascinating. How might a scientist explain it?

A: There is no man alone, because every man is a microcosm, and carries the whole world about him. (Browne)

1119. Q: I once heard a most interesting remark at a lecture. The speaker said that the greater the neurosis, the greater can be the swing over to the side of mental health, providing the individual works hard on himself. Where might this swing to sanity start?

A: If you are content with the old world, try to preserve it; it is sick . . . But if you can no longer live in the eternal conflict between your convictions and life, thinking one way and acting another, take it upon yourselves to leave the shelter of the pale and ruinous arches. (Herzen)

1120. Q: This calls for a personal declaration of freedom.

A: It is time to explain myself — let us stand up. (Whitman)

1121. Q: I want to leave the disastrous battleground of society, but need more power than I now possess.

A: How great is the power of truth! Of its own power it can easily defend itself against all the ingenuity of cunning and wisdom of men, and against the treacherous plots of all the world. (Cicero)

1122. Q: What fundamental understanding can establish us in new powers in the most efficient manner?

A: Men have but to understand this: they must cease to care for material and external matters . . . let them apply one hundredth part of the energy now used by them in out-

ward concerns to those in which they are free — to the recognition and profession of the truth that confronts them, to the
deliverance of themselves and others from the falsehoods
which conceal the truth. Then the false system of life which
now torments us, which threatens us with still greater suffering, will be destroyed at once without struggle, then the
Kingdom of Heaven, at least in that first stage . . . will be
established. (Tolstoy)

The way out of the wilderness

1123. Q: Please explain the difference between a receptive
mind and a gullible mind.

A: There is an old simile in India that if you place a
cup of milk before a *Raja Hamsa* (swan) with plenty of water
in it, he will take all the milk and leave the water. In that way
we should take what is of value in knowledge, and leave the
dross. (Vivekananda)

1124. Q: My study has revealed a definite connection
between self-responsibility and self-happiness.

A: To be happy means to be self-sufficient. (Aristotle)

1125. Q: My aim is to toss aside everything useless, and to
cut a straight path through the mental wilderness, to break
out into clear ground. Will you provide a way?

A: Many have puzzled themselves about the origin of
evil. I am content to observe that there is evil, and that there
is a way to escape from it; and with this I begin and end.
(Newton)

1126. Q: It is unfortunately true that many of us are like
forged paintings; we look good, but are often valueless. What
original values can we reclaim?

A: How are we constituted by Nature? To be free, to
be noble, to be modest. (Epictetus)

1127. Q: You have said that a truly spiritual man has a
certain indifference about him, which radiates itself as

strength. What is an example?

A: The only way to get the confidence of the world is to show the world that you do not want their confidence. (Haydon)

1128. *Q*: Is it better for us to stick to one authentic teacher or to see what all of them have to say?

A: Does not a bee gather honey out of many flowers? (Boehme)

1129. *Q*: I am gradually awakening to the need to break out of my self-centred world, and also sense the power to do it. Apparently, an authentic need creates the very capacity for fulfilling the need.

A: The first breath of spiritual life is indeed, in one sense, the realization of this capacity, but in another sense, it is only the beginning of a realization which is itself incapable of limitation . . . we have in us the power to transcend the bounds of our narrow individuality, and to find ourselves in that which seems to lie beyond us. (Caird)

1130. *Q*: My best achievement up to now is to clearly see that there are a thousand reasons for wrestling with these ideas and not one good reason for ignoring them.

A: Pure gold! (Blake)

Profitable principles in summary

a. Every person possesses a storehouse of hidden power.
b. As our deeper mind awakens, our sleeping energies emerge.
c. Every unhappy event can be used to discover new powers.
d. Place a supreme value on all these principles.
e. Awareness of a negativity provides power over it.
f. Nothing can prevent you from becoming a new person.
g. Look in an entirely new direction for a refreshed life!
h. Take very good care of your spiritual prosperity.
i. Naturalness is an available and a supreme power.
j. Think of all the good reasons for seeking self-newness.

16. You Can Now Conquer Fear and Depression

1131. *Q*: I am a far more frightened person than I appear to be before others. How can I dissolve my fears?

A: If men who do not understand life would only approach nearer to the phantoms which alarm them, and would examine them, they would see that they are only phantoms, and not realities. (Tolstoy)

1132. *Q*: I feel depressed because I am unable to correct all the mistakes I have made.

A: Do not cumber yourself with fruitless pains to mend and remedy remote effects; let the soul be erect, and all things will go well. (Emerson)

1133. *Q*: Please make us aware of a negative influence we should guard against.

A: Let not that which in another is contrary to nature be an evil to you, for you are not made by nature to be depressed with others, nor to be unhappy with others, but to be happy with them. (Epictetus)

1134. *Q*: Sometimes I feel cut off from everything that is right and good and necessary. Is that a false feeling?

A: We are not cast away, not separate. (Plotinus)

1135. *Q*: How can we put more life into our living?

A: The millions are awake enough for physical labour; but only one in a million is awake enough for effective intellectual exertion, only one in a hundred millions to a poetic or divine life. To be awake is to be alive . . . We must learn to reawaken and keep ourselves awake, not by mechanical aids, but by an infinite expectation of the dawn. (Thoreau)

1136. *Q*: We are unable to get to the point about anything, especially our problems. How can we live simply, directly, without fuss and without discussion?

A: A cucumber is bitter? Throw it away. There are briars in the road? Turn aside from them. This is enough. Do not add, 'Why were such things made in the world?' (Aurelius)

1137. *Q*: So a main problem is our own mental wanderings!

A: We must get rid of all this nonsense. (Kierkegaard)

1138. *Q*: May we have a specific instance of wasteful thinking?

A: The individual fears ridicule above all things, and ridicule is the certain result of originality. No one, therefore, wishes to make a party of his own; everyone wishes to be on the side of all the world. (Amiel)

1139. *Q*: Please provide a basic fact about genuine happiness.

A: The happiness we receive from ourselves is greater than that which we obtain from our surroundings. (Metrodorus)

1140. *Q*: It is sometimes discouraging to see how many things we do not know.

A: The only useful question in this matter is this: how a man may know that he is in the way of regeneration, that he is spiritually alive, and growing in the inward and new man. (Law)

There is no fear in love

1141. *Q*: I feel myself almost in possession of lasting contentment, but the secret is still inches from my grasp.

A: Whether we are in a pleasant or a painful state depends, finally, upon the kind of matter that pervades and engrosses our consciousness. (Schopenhauer)

1142. *Q*: Then authentic peace can come only from authentic spirituality?

A: In the highest stage of divine comfort is that peace which is said to pass all understanding. (Tauler)

1143. *Q*: We have been advised to root out fear in order to love and be loved. Please explain.

A: No man loves the man whom he fears. (Aristotle)

1144. *Q*: Authentic love conquers all things, including fear and trembling?

A: There is no fear in love; but perfect love casteth out fear. (New Testament)

1145. *Q*: It is said that psychic power is altogether different from the power of human authority. Will you please clarify?

A: The man who fears nothing is as powerful as he who is feared by everybody. (Schiller)

1146. *Q*: Much of our enthusiasm is like a boomerang that falls back to strike us as depression. Please provide us with an enthusiasm that goes places.

A: I pray thee, O God, that I may be beautiful within. (Socrates)

1147. *Q*: I feel a particular kind of frustration. For years I have tried to succeed by imitating the methods of people who have already won their objectives. I sometimes hope that tomorrow will be the turning point, but another part of me senses that I am going about it all wrong.

A: Is it not then high time to look out for some better ground to stand upon, than such learning as this? (Law)

1148. *Q*: But I do not know any other way.

A: There is a kind of elevation which does not depend on fortune. It is a certain air which distinguishes us, and seems to destine us for great things; it is a price which we set upon ourselves. (La Rochefoucauld)

1149. *Q*: And this sets us free of the anxiety involved in wanting things from others?

A: I care not so much what I am in the opinion of others, as what I am in my own. I would be rich of myself, and not by borrowing. (Montaigne)

1150. *Q*: I wonder whether I can express my problem clearly. My mind takes over and forces me to think stupid and useless thoughts. I am like a man swept along by a raging river, battered and miserable, with no way out. Do you understand my condition?

A: Man is so made that by continually telling him he is a fool he believes it, and by continually telling it to himself he makes himself believe it. For man holds an inward talk with himself, which it pays him to regulate . . . We must keep silent as much as possible, and talk with ourselves only of God, whom we know to be true, and thus we convince ourselves of the truth. (Pascal)

Have no anxiety over results

1151. *Q*: Our study group is at present exploring false escapes from fear and tension. I believe you include most social activities as a wrong route.

A: I have said that people are rendered sociable by their inability to endure solitude, that is to say, their own society. They become sick of themselves. Their mind is wanting in flexibility; it has no movement of its own, so they try to give it some — by drink, for instance . . . They are always looking for some form of excitement, of the strongest kind they can bear — the excitement of being with people of like nature with themselves; and if they fail in this, their mind sinks by its own weight, and they fall into grievous lethargy. (Schopenhauer)

1152. Q: What is the matter with people who constantly chase from one place to another, from one activity to the next, in a vain attempt to find satisfaction?

A: They see not good so near. (Pythagoras)

1153. Q: Why do we fail to see how easily we are fooled by the outer world?

A: Oh, the difficulty of fixing the attention of men on the world within them! (Coleridge)

1154. Q: What idea can fix our attention on our inner riches?

A: Why do you look without for that which is within you? (Eckhart)

1155. Q: I would appreciate having a thought to call upon whenever I feel discouraged over my self-work.

A: Nothing is more delightful than the light of truth. (Cicero)

1156. Q: What truth would help a person who feels he has failed to be a success in his career or work?

A: Nature has not said to me, 'Be not poor,' still less, 'Be rich.' She calls out to me, 'Be independent!' (Chamfort)

1157. Q: What does a man gain by following this counsel?

A: He is independent of everybody and everything. Always do your duty, but without attachment to it. That is how a man reaches ultimate truth — by working without anxiety about results. (Hinduism)

1158. Q: There is a certain fear which many people never speak about, probably because they are unaware of it. What is your comment on the fear of being alone?

A: A wise man is never less alone than when he is alone. (Swift)

1159. Q: What is the way of the wise man?

A: I must be myself. I cannot break myself any longer for you, or you. If you can love me for what I am, we shall be the happier. If you cannot . . . I will not hurt you and myself by hypocritical attentions. If you are true, but not in the same truth with me, cleave to your own companions; I will seek my own. I do this not selfishly but humbly and truly. It is alike your interest, and mine, and all men's, however long we have dwelt in lies, to live in truth. Does this sound harsh today? You will soon love what is dictated by your nature as well as mine, and if we follow the truth it will bring us out safe at last. (Emerson)

1160. *Q*: Can we really escape our anxieties?

A: Like birds escaped from the net. (Buddhism)

How to be free of all fears

1161. *Q*: Sometimes I feel like a man adrift in a boat in a foggy sea. I don't know where I am going or what is happening to me.

A: Fear not . . . there is no danger for you. There is a way to cross over the ocean of the world, and by this way the wise men have reached the shore. This same way I point out to you, for it is the way to destroy the world's fear. Crossing the ocean of the world by this way, you will win perfect peace. (Shankara)

1162. *Q*: In a single sentence, why does humanity go from one disaster to another?

A: If you are surprised at the number of our maladies, count our cooks. (Seneca)

1163. *Q*: But public leaders seem so sure of themselves.

A: Nothing is so firmly believed as what we least know. (Montaigne)

1164. *Q*: Then there must be no hero-worship, even in spiritual matters?

A: None are superior to what you might become. (Balzac)

1165. *Q*: My studies are beginning to lift certain kinds of depression which haunted me for years. What esoteric law explains this?

A: Apprehensions are greater in proportion as things are unknown. (Livy)

1166. *Q*: I wish to be totally free of fear. Can spiritual mental health, in its highest form, provide this perfection?

A: God hath not given us the spirit of fear; but of power, and of love, and of a sound mind. (New Testament)

1167. *Q*: Does our climb to these peaks of truth save us from a secret fear of punishment?

A: He who ascends to this height has all things under his feet. (Ruysbroeck)

1168. *Q*: I would like to start climbing.

A: Come forth, and bring with you a heart that watches and receives. (Wordsworth)

1169. *Q*: I notice that the sages call our for personal receptivity, honest receptivity, while cautioning us against merely toying with the truth. Please comment.

A: If a foolish man is associated with a wise man, even all his life, the foolish man will understand truth as little as a spoon understands the taste of soup. (Buddhism)

1170. *Q*: The mystics point out that unenlightened man is split into dozens of separate and contradictory parts which battle endlessly with each other. Observation proves the truth of this. What technique can bring a man together into oneness, wholeness?

A: Man need not perform any acts or exploits, but has only to make an intense effort at consciousness. (Tolstoy)

1171. Q: It is certain that our frenzied activities — even our so-called noble ones — are self-deceiving attempts to escape from our miserable selves, but what else can we do?

A: I will not move until I have the highest command ... Your virtuous projects, so called, do not cheer me. I know that which shall come will cheer me. If I cannot work, at least I need not lie. All that is clearly due today is not to lie. (Emerson)

Be your own good fortune!

1172. Q: As all of us know by experience, the truth seems frightening, but at the same time it is the only force capable of banishing fear. Will you go into this?

A: A little boy wearing the mask of a lion looks quite fierce. He runs out where his little sister is playing and shrieks out in a horrible voice, which shocks and terrifies his sister, making her cry out in terror, and making her attempt to escape from the frightening creature. But when her brother takes off his mask, she runs back to exclaim, 'It is my nice brother after all!' (Ramakrishna)

1173. Q: I am apprehensive that others won't like me.

A: From a distance it is something; nearby it is nothing. (La Fontaine)

1174. Q: How can I quickly recover from an upset or a depression?

A: When you have been compelled by circumstances to be disturbed in any manner, quickly return to yourself, and do not continue out of tune longer than the compulsion lasts. You will have increasing control over your own harmony by continually returning to it. (Aurelius)

1175. Q: What can create self-encouragement?

A: There is always hope in a man that actually and earnestly works. In idleness alone is there perpetual despair. (Carlyle)

1176. *Q*: Please point out a cause of anxiety of which we may be unaware.

A: We often try to banish the gloom and despondency of the present by speculating upon our chances of success in the future; a process which leads us to invent a great many unreal hopes. Every one of them contains the seed of illusion, and disappointment is inevitable when our hopes are shattered. (Schopenhauer)

1177. *Q*: You say that man lives almost entirely in flattering self-pictures of being good, rather than in the genuine article. This would seem to be a major cause of tension, for he must endlessly try to protect his illusory images.

A: That virtue which requires to be ever guarded is scarcely worth the sentinel. (Goldsmith)

1178. *Q*: I have been both startled and helped by realizing how much we live from unrealistic self-pictures of ourselves. How would you describe a man living like this?

A: The slave and prisoner of his own opinion of himself. (Thoreau)

1179. *Q*: Please show us how to be free from the chains of opinion.

A: I call that mind free which protects itself against the usurpations of society, which does not cower to human opinion, which feels itself accountable to a higher tribunal than man's, which respects itself too much to be the slave or tool of the many or the few. (Channing)

1180. *Q*: You have said that the man who knows the truth from himself has no need for frantic belief. Please explain.

A: Would it not be absurd and disrespectful if you were in the presence of a king to say to him, 'Sir, I believe your majesty is here'? (Molinos)

1181. *Q*: So we need only to *see* what we already possess?

A: Henceforth I ask not good-fortune, I myself am

good-fortune. (Whitman)

How to erase secret faults

1182. *Q*: I feel myself capable of winning this new life, but at the same time I possess secret faults which threaten to rise up and expose me. This frustrates my efforts.

A: Let nothing, therefore, deter a well minded soul from persevering with fervour in this firm resolution. No, not the sight of her daily defect, imperfections, or sins, or remorses for them; but rather let her increase in courage even from her falls, and from the experience of her own impotency let her be incited to run more earnestly . . . she will be enabled to do all things and conquer all resistances. (Baker)

1183. *Q*: What can we ask of life without fearing that it will answer with a *no*?

A: He who asks of life nothing but the improvement of his own nature, and a continuous good progress towards inner contentment and spiritual submission, is less likely than anyone else to miss and waste life. (Amiel)

1184. *Q*: I am increasingly aware of the error of compromising with what is truly right for me. What esoteric principle covers this?

A: No man can serve two masters. (Jesus)

1185. *Q*: We could use detailed advice for not compromising, for standing up for ourselves in the right way.

A: The characteristic of heroism is its persistency. All men have wandering impulses, fits and starts . . . But when you have chosen your part, abide by it, and do not weakly try to reconcile yourself with the world. The heroic cannot be the common, nor the common the heroic. (Emerson)

1186. *Q*: My work at the business office is a major cause of tension and pressure.

A: Carry religious principles into common life...
Soon business, with all its cares and anxieties, the whole
'unprofitable stir and fever of the world' will be to us a thing
of the past. (Caird)

1187. *Q*: I am highly encouraged by realizing that we can be
in the world but not snared by it.

A: Heaven is under our feet as well as over our heads.
(Thoreau)

1188. *Q*: Our false activities are evident enough, for our
inner nature suffers from them constantly. Please recommend
a healthy activity which serves our true needs.

A: To build up that strength of mind which appre-
hends and cleaves to great universal truths, is the highest
intellectual culture. (Channing)

1189. *Q*: The great teachers say that evil is really a state of
hypnosis, of ignorance and unconsciousness. How can a
person tell whether he dwells in this psychic sleep?

A: No evil man is happy. (Juvenal)

1190. *Q*: I never mention it to anyone, but I am secretly
afraid of angry people. I go out of my way to please others so
as to not arouse their hostility. I hope something can be done
about this uncomfortable condition.

A: The man who is just and resolute will not be moved
from his settled purpose, either by the misdirected rage of his
fellow citizens, or by the threats of an imperious tyrant.
(Horace)

Secrets for self-success

1191. *Q*: As a school teacher, I wish to show my students
how immodesty and arrogance bring self-punishment. Do you
have a lesson I might use?

A: It is the tall pine which is cruelly shaken by the
wind, and the lofty towers that fall so heavily, and the high-

est peaks which are struck by the storm. (Schopenhauer)

1192. *Q*: How can I avoid getting upset over the unpleasant words and acts of others?

A: Inquire of yourself as soon as you awaken from sleep whether it will make any difference to you, if another does or does not do what is just and right. It will make no difference. (Aurelius)

1193. *Q*: You teach that inner dawning comes only after we have been disillusioned, when we start to doubt our traditional beliefs, and when we have lost our supposed securities. Will you please review this?

A: To understand things we must have been once in them and then have come out of them; so that first there must be captivity and then deliverance, illusion followed by disillusion, enthusiasm by disappointment. He who is still under the spell, and he who has never felt the spell, are equally incompetent. We only know well what we have first believed, then judged. To understand we must be free, yet not have been always free. (Amiel)

1194. *Q*: What happens to a man as a result of this experience?

A: How changed from him whom we knew! (Virgil)

1195. *Q*: I have collected and studied mystical books for twenty years. There is a definite difference and superiority in them, unlike anything found in books of ordinary religion and psychology. What causes the difference?

A: If a book comes from the heart, it will contrive to reach other hearts. (Carlyle)

1196. *Q*: Nervous people are usually advised to get involved with something, or to forget themselves by helping others. While this does seem to be stale and mechanical advice, doesn't it work for people?

A: Take away their diversion, and you will see them

dried up with weariness. They feel then their nothingness without knowing it . . . If our condition were truly happy, we would not need diversion. (Pascal)

1197. Q: If diversion fails, what succeeds?

A: Gently, but with undeniable will, divesting myself of the holds that would hold me. (Whitman)

1198. Q: What is the cause of suddenly finding ourselves in trouble?

A: The cause is sleep or forgetfulness: some sleep when they should keep awake, and some forget when they should remember. And this is the very cause why often at the resting-places some pilgrims, in some things, come off losers. Pilgrims should watch, and remember what they have already received. (Bunyan)

1199. Q: I have already received so much valuable aid I am eager to push on with the inner journey.

A: I applaud your devotion to philosophy, I rejoice to hear that your spirit has set sail, like the returning Ulysses, for its native land — that glorious, that only real country — the world of unseen truth. (Plotinus)

The truth is a solid rock

1200. Q: Please comment on right and wrong attitudes towards these principles.

A: It is clear that the first step in the new birth is a reception of truths by the understanding, and the second is the will to act in accordance with truths, and finally to practise them. No one, however, can be said to be reformed by mere knowledge of truth; for man is able to acquire these and to talk about, teach, and preach them . . . But he is a reformed man who has an affection for truth for the sake of truth. (Swedenborg)

1201. Q: How does an awakened man show affection for what is right?

A: The subject on which I meditate is truth. The practice to which I devote myself is truth. The topic of my conversation is truth. My thoughts are always in the truth. For lo! my self has become the truth. (Buddha)

1202. *Q*: You teach that self-knowledge and cosmic knowledge dissolves all conflict, but I can't get over the notion that I must fight fiercely against a hostile world.

A: Cast away your opinion and you are saved. Who hinders you from casting it away? (Aurelius)

1203. *Q*: Nothing is clearer to me than that the man who masquerades as a policeman will be afraid of meeting a real policeman. I want to drop pretence and be a real person, which I believe is a right desire.

A: Now this is nothing else but the superior light giving light to the understanding, so that the human understanding becomes divine, made one with the divine. (Yepes)

1204. *Q*: And this oneness is the same as love?

A: Egotism erects its centre in itself; love places it out of itself in the axis of the universal whole. Love aims at unity, egotism at solitude. Love is the citizen ruler of a flourishing republic, egotism is a despot in a devastated land. (Schiller)

1205. *Q*: We are afraid because we seem so small when compared to the mighty universe.

A: What frightens you? Stand then and be free. If the sun come down, the moons crumble into dust, systems after systems are hurled into annihilation, what is that to you? Stand as a rock; you are indestructible . . . so break this chain and be free for ever. What frightens you, what holds you down? It is only ignorance and delusion; nothing else can bind you . . . Therefore, if you dare, stand on that. (Vivekananda)

1206. *Q*: So by daring to stand, a man actually learns to stand?

A: I will liken him unto a wise man, which built his house upon a rock. And the rain descended, and the floods came, and the winds blew, and beat upon that house; and it fell not: for it was founded upon a rock. (Jesus)

1207. *Q*: When does this become our state?

A: When we rise above ourselves. (Caird)

1208. *Q*: These ideas are new to me, but at the same time are interesting and refreshing.

A: Come on, then, and let us go together, and let us spend our time in discoursing of things that are profitable. (Bunyan)

Think about the following guides

a. You can completely dissolve all kinds of fears.
b. The self-awakened person is the unafraid person.
c. Depression is merely a misunderstanding of your nature.
d. Chase out negative thoughts the moment they try to enter.
e. You need have no concern over results in exterior affairs.
f. Nature has not made you to be anxious about anything.
g. All we need to do is to be courageously honest.
h. You can become your own good fortune!
i. Never be influenced by another man's negativity.
j. Practise at standing unafraid and you will stand unafraid.

17. Cosmic Principles for Help and Guidance

1209. *Q*: Your invitation to explore the new and the unknown has aroused me to new life. What is the single most helpful fact about our exploration of inner space?

A: It is good to love the unknown. (Lamb)

1210. *Q*: What is the principal power a man needs for living his own life, for being independent of the quarrels and the neuroses of others?

A: A singular strength of mind is therefore required to enable a man to live among others consistently with his own ideas and convictions, to be master of himself, and not fall into the habits or exhibit the same passions as those with whom he associates. (Spinoza)

1211. *Q*: Please refresh our minds on the overwhelming need for self-examination and self-study.

A: He that knows himself, knows others; and he that is ignorant of himself, could not write a very profound lecture on other men's heads. (Colton)

1212. *Q*: How much time should we put into self-study?

A: Can one desire too much of a good thing? (Cervantes)

1213. *Q*: Please explain the process by which these ideas become a man's own living truths.

A: The bees visit the flowers here and there, but they make honey of them which is all their own; it is no longer

thyme or marjoram: so the pieces borrowed from others he
will transform and mix up into a work all his own.
(Montaigne)

1214. Q: Now that you have made me aware of the artificial
contentment in which most people live, I no longer want to
bear its burden. Please provide some basic information about
this false peace.

A: Many are secretly seeking their own ends in what
they do, yet know it not. They seem to live in good peace of
mind so long as things go well with them, and according to
their desires, but if their desires be frustrated, immediately
they are shaken and displeased. (Kempis)

1215. Q: To review, esoteric medicine is ready for the patient
as soon as the patient is ready for it.

A: What is the use of the most sovereign of medicines
while they stand on the sick man's table? What is the
mightiest of truths so long as it is not believed? The
spiritually sick still mocks at the medicine offered; he will
not know its cure. (MacDonald)

1216. Q: All of us know that something is wrong, but we are
heartened by hearing that healing is available.

A: Seeking the way, you must exert yourselves and
strive with diligence . . . free yourselves from the tangled net
of sorrow. Walk in the path with steadfast aim. A sick man
may be cured by the healing power of medicine and will be
rid of all his ailments without beholding the physician.
(Buddha)

Esoteric teachings are courageous

1217. Q: I now realize that things like fame or a college
education are not automatic signs of a man's intelligence, but
I still do not know how to judge a man's mental level, including my own.

A: It is no proof of a man's understanding to be able
to confirm whatever he pleases; but to be able to discern that

what is true is true, and that what is false is false; this is the mark and character of intelligence. (Emerson)

1218. Q: It is apparent that foolish and incompetent men often receive the greatest public honours. Why?

A: The world more often rewards the appearances of merit than it does merit itself. (La Rochefoucauld)

1219. Q: Please comment upon the winning of spiritual insight.

A: As to the thirst after knowledge, it is an old law that we all get whatever we want. None of us can get anything other than what we fix our hearts upon . . . The success sometimes may come immediately, but we must be ready to wait patiently even for what may look like an infinite length of time. The student who sets out with such a spirit of perseverance will surely find success and realization at last. (Vivekananda)

1220. Q: Esotericism seems to call for a totally new kind of rebellion; not the usual rebellion which asserts itself egotistically in public for selfish gains, but rebellion against all forms of falsehood, including our own self-punishing errors. Please confirm.

A: I have no inclination to assault myself; it would be of no use. You may do it yourselves if you choose — I refuse. (Tolstoy)

1221. Q: News reports usually consist of the foolish and the bad actions of men. Please give us some cheerful news.

A: Money is not required to buy one necessity of the soul (Thoreau)

1222. Q: There is a refreshing courage and honesty about these teachings. They are not hiding anything, as many man-made doctrines do. They tell us to take no one's word for anything, but to prove all things for ourselves.

A: You may proceed at once with the proof, as I

readily grant you this. (Plato)

1223. *Q*: I have noticed how people usually ask the same questions, for instance, everyone wants to know how to up-lift his fortunes. Will you please discuss another often-asked question?

A: I may be asked what I mean by Inward Spiritual Freedom ... Spiritual freedom is the attribute of a mind in which reason and conscience have begun to act, and which is free through its own energy, through fidelity to the truth, through resistance to temptation ... We are in the midst of influences which menace the intellect and heart; and to be free is to withstand and conquer these. (Channing)

1224. *Q*: As we toss out false maps in life, what takes their place?

A: Directions for leading a happy life. (Horace)

1225. *Q*: Most of us are so timid about changing our ways, even our unhappy ways. We wonder what will happen to us if we dare to go against the lashing waves of social custom to launch out on our own voyage.

A: You have no business with consequences; you are to tell the truth. (Johnson)

Your psychic sight is everything

1226. *Q*: We are told that self-newness comes as we practise self-awareness, as we observe ourselves. What does this mean?

A: Whatever you do, act always in full presence of mind. Be thoughtful in eating and drinking, in walking or standing, in sleeping or waking, while talking or being silent. (Buddha)

1227. *Q*: We are advised to concentrate our powers of mental attention on worthwhile objects, like noticing the nature of our passing thoughts. What is a type of wasted attention?

A: How much trouble he avoids who does not look to

see what his neighbour says or does or thinks, but only what he does himself, that it may be just and pure. (Aurelius)

1228. Q: I find it helpful to write down and think about a new principle each day. May I have one for tomorrow?

A: It is the mind that makes us rich and happy, in whatever conditions we are, and money signifies no more to it than it does to the gods. (Seneca)

1229. Q: Then the correction of our psychic sight is everything? For example, will we then see the availability of all we need for the lofty life?

A: What man is there of you, whom if his son asks for bread, will he give him a stone? (Jesus)

1230. Q: We have a problem. People say they are hungry, but cannot find bread. Mysticism says people are hungry all right, but refuse to recognize and accept bread. What can be done?

A: Open up your inward sense, and see and hear. (Suso)

1231. Q: It would be much easier for me if I understood human nature better. Is it true that like attracts like, and if so, how does it work?

A: Take the case of a large number of people who have gathered together for the purpose of carrying out some practical project. If there are two rascals among them, they will recognize each other quickly, as if each wore a similar badge, and they will at once conspire for some selfishness or treachery . . . It is really curious to see how two such men, especially if they are morally and intellectually inferior, will recognize each other at first sight, with what zeal they will try to become friends, how affably and cheerfully they will rush to greet each other. (Schopenhauer)

1232. Q: Why is it so many people can attract our attention, but few can win our affection?

A: Hearts may be attracted by assumed qualities, but

the affections are only to be fixed by those which are real.
(Moy)

1233. Q: It is a great relief from false responsibility towards
others to hear that a man must place his own mental
maturity before everything else. I believe you mean that we
can never give more goodness than that which we actually
possess in ourselves.

A: You will be of as much worth to others as you are
to yourself. (Cicero)

1234. Q: Mankind seems unable to see the benefit in being
true to himself and to the universal plan surrounding him.

A: It's wiser being good than bad . . . It's fitter being
sane than mad. (Browning)

How to know what you need to know

1235. Q: The mystic masters state that we stand in our own
way, but also say we can cease to be self-blocked. Please
provide an example of these two points.

A: So long, therefore, as we are not agitated by passions which are contrary to our nature, so long is the power
of the soil by which it seeks to understand things not
impeded; and so long, therefore, has it the power of forming
clear and distinct ideas. (Spinoza)

1236. Q: In a few words, how can we rescue ourselves from
ourselves?

A: We can only cure our tendency downwards by the
power that leads upwards . . . by a total conversion to the
divine law. (Hierocles)

1237. Q: How can we practise authentic self-interest?

A: By neglecting self-interest we achieve self-interest.
(Lao-tse)

1238. Q: I don't understand this.

A: Self-interest is but the survival of the animal in us. Humanity only begins for man with self-surrender. (Amiel)

1239. *Q*: That resembles the New Testament idea that we must first lose ourselves in order to find ourselves. It seems paradoxical.

A: The truest sayings are paradoxical. (Taoism)

1240. *Q*: It is fascinating to hear that we can know everything we need to know for an abundant life. How does this come about?

A: The more a man has unity and simplicity in himself, the more things and the deeper things he understands, and that without labour, because he receives the light and understanding from above. (Kempis)

1241. *Q*: Our class in esotericism is compiling a list of basic spiritual laws which we intend to study with special care. Please contribute a fundamental principle for human relations.

A: The slanderer is like one who flings dust at another when the wind is contrary; the dust does but return on him who threw it. The virtuous man cannot be hurt and the misery that the other would inflict comes back on himself. (Buddha)

1242. *Q*: You have said that the desire for inner awakening starts the good work. What is the end of this healthy yearning?

A: When this desire is alive, and breaks forth in any creature under heaven, then the lost sheep is found. (Law)

1243. *Q*: What a fantastic victory would be ours if we could avoid problems and defeats before they occur! Does the regaining of our psychic sight confer on us the power to foresee and escape misfortune?

A: The tempest threatens before it rises upon us; buildings creak before they fall to pieces. (Seneca)

1244. *Q*: Is it true that the truth is always trying to attract our attention, but we fail to see it because of our trifling distractions?

A: I always feel as if someone was calling me, and I must look around, and I keep looking around. (Auerbach)

1245. *Q*: What do the mystics see that we do not?

A: Great men are they who see that spiritual is stronger than any material force, that thoughts rule the world. (Emerson)

Esotericism provides true mental health

1246. *Q*: When we see public authorities squabbling with each other from opposite corners, it is apparent that most human beings do not really understand what life is all about. How can an individual seeker refuse all this childishness and advance to a conscious perception of life?

A: The worst of human errors spring in most cases from the fact that men who stand on a low intellectual level, when they encounter events of a higher order, instead of trying to rise to the higher level from which these events can be rightly viewed, and making an effort to understand them, judge them by their own low standards, and the less they know of what they speak, the more arrogant and fixed are their judgments. (Tolstoy)

1247. *Q*: I notice how you repeatedly urge us to work for a clear and an understanding mind. Please start us in the right direction.

A: Whatsoever things are true, whatsoever things are honest, whatsoever things are just, whatsoever things are pure, whatsoever things are lovely, whatsoever things are of good report; if there be any virtue, and if there be any praise, think on these things. (New Testament)

1248. *Q*: Because I now see that our major aim is to have a clear mind, my inner work is much easier and smoother.

A: To see clearly is poetry, prophecy, and religion — all in one. (Ruskin)

1249. *Q*: May we have an example of a sorrow which ceases to exist to a highly conscious human being?

A: The happy never say, and never hear said, farewell. (Landor)

1250. *Q*: What should we do with our lives?

A: The truth is the end and aim of all existence, and the worlds originate so that the truth may come and dwell therein. Those who fail to aspire for the truth have missed the purpose of life. Blessed is he who rests in the truth. (Buddhism)

1251. *Q*: What lesson is needed by someone who is timid in taking the initiative towards his own development?

A: The bell never rings of itself; unless someone handles or moves it, it is silent. (Plautus)

1252. *Q*: I am surprised at a recent discovery I have made while talking with people about truth and reality. Many people get tense and defensive, as if they see the truth as an enemy, instead of as a friend.

A: The man who comes into the world with the notion that he is really going to instruct it in matters of the highest importance, may thank his stars if he escapes with a whole skin. (Schopenhauer)

1253. *Q*: This explains why we must depend upon ourselves for spiritual advancement, not upon useless public organizations.

A: The world is his who can see through its pretension. (Emerson)

1254. *Q*: Mystical and religious teachers often use lofty terms to describe the other kind of life, such as referring to it as the kingdom of heaven. Will you please describe this same state in everyday language?

A: Health of mind. (Cicero)

How to have daily inspiration

1255. *Q*: I belong to a small group which studies these principles. May I have an idea for discussion at our next meeting?

A: Public opinion is a weak tyrant compared with our own private opinion. What a man thinks of himself, that it is which determines, or rather indicates, his fate. (Thoreau)

1256. *Q*: So to be loyal to ourselves, we must cease to be loyal to all the surrounding follies.

A: A hero must not allow himself to be outwardly bound; he must resist everything by his inward strength. (Auerbach)

1257. *Q*: I am like a tennis player who swings in the same place every time, regardless of where the ball arrives. I need to awaken my flexibility in handling daily events.

A: Prudence is that virtue by which we discern what is proper to be done under the various circumstances of time and place. (Milton)

1258. *Q*: By prudence I believe you mean this higher kind of spiritual insight which comes with self-knowledge.

A: Learning dissipates many doubts, and causes many things otherwise invisible to be seen. (Sufism)

1259. *Q*: Esoterically, what is the life of personal safety?

A: You will never come to harm in the practice of virtue. (Plato)

1260. *Q*: What can be done when we feel that the obstacles to this new life are stronger than our powers for progress?

A: Cannot a strong interest turn difficulty into pleasure? Let the love of truth, of which I have spoken, be awakened, and obstacles in the way to it will whet, not discourage, the mind, and inspire a new delight into its acquisition. (Channing)

1261. *Q*: What should we do if we stumble along the path?

A: Lose no time, get up and take the course again, for he who rises quickly and continues his race makes it as if he had never fallen. (Molinos)

1262. *Q*: There must be a wisely efficient way to achieve the maximum benefit from these ideas in minimum time.

A: Ramakrishna used to tell a story of some men who went into a mango orchard and busied themselves in counting the leaves, the twigs, and the branches, examining their colour, comparing their size, and noting down everything most carefully, and then got up a learned discussion on each of these topics . . . But one of them, more sensible than the others, did not care for all these things, and instead thereof, began to eat the mango fruit. And was he not wise?So leave this counting of leaves and twigs and this notetaking to others . . . You can never once see a strong spiritual man among these 'leaf-counters'. (Vivekananda)

1263. *Q*: It is an esoteric principle to use everything as a means of regaining our self-authority. Please mention an area we can use.

A: What is the true test of character, unless it be its progressive development in the bustle and turmoil, in the action and reaction of daily life? (Goethe)

1264. *Q*: It would help me to have a foremost rule to practise in all circumstances.

A: What is a man's first duty? The answer's brief: To be himself. (Ibsen)

Influence yourself for good!

1265. *Q*: What determines whether we influence ourselves for good or for defeat?

A: Your real influence is measured by your treatment of yourself. (Alcott)

1266. Q: Please give us a self-treating thought for good.

A: Renouncing the honours at which the world aims, I
desire only to know the truth . . . and to the maximum of my
power, I exhort all other men to do the same. (Plato)

1267. Q: What advice could I give to someone who is obsessed with the need to become popular and famous?

A: It matters not what you are thought to be, but
what you are. (Syrus)

1268. Q: Human optimism of one day is smashed by the
disasters of the next day. What reliable optimism is offered
by the mystic masters?

A: Is not the truth the truth? (Shakespeare)

1269. Q: I feel that the truth about life cannot be found on
either side of human arguments, for instance, religious or
political arguments, but is located above them. Am I on the
right track?

A: Whenever opposite views are held with warmth by
religious-minded men, we may take it for granted there is
some higher truth which embraces both. All high truth is the
union of two contradictions. (Robertson)

1270. Q: Please confirm the following statement. We often
assume we have found the truth, when in fact, we have
merely gazed once more upon our old and self-centred
opinions, for the truth is above our habitual thinking.

A: All men who know not where to look for truth,
save in the narrow well of self, will find their own image at
the bottom, and mistake it for what they are seeking.
(Lowell)

1271. Q: You say that honest awareness of self-division is the
beginning of healing, of wholeness. I do not understand this,
but wish to do so.

A: The very emergence of the contradiction in our
consciousness is at the same time the silent prophecy of its

solution . . . that which knows or feels division or discord must be a unity which transcends division or discord . . . it is a consciousness in which the contradiction or discord vanishes. (Caird)

1272. *Q*: When we have banished self-division, when we know our true nature, do we then truly understand what life is all about?

A: When a man knows this, potentially he knows all things. (MacDonald)

1273. *Q*: And this new nature is the basis of authentic compassion?

A: I love all men. I know that at bottom they cannot be otherwise, and under all the false and overloaded and glittering masquerade, there is, in every man, a noble nature beneath; only they cannot bring it out, and whatever they do that is false and cunning and evil, there still remains the sentence of our Great Example: 'Forgive them, for they know not what they do.' (Auerbach)

1274. *Q*: It is interesting how a truth suddenly strikes into our consciousness. Yesterday, for the first time, I saw why only a self-unified man can reach down to help others.

A: When the full corn is in the ear, it bends down because it is full. (Cecil)

A dynamic reminder for you

1275. *Q*: It seems we must concern ourselves with two major facts — that something is very wrong, but right personal effort can make everything right. Will you restate that in your own words?

A: The world is built for the truth, but false combinations of thought misrepresent the true state of things and bring forth errors. Errors can be fashioned as it pleases those who cherish them, therefore they are pleasant to look upon, but they are unstable and contain the seeds of dissolution. Truth cannot be fashioned . . . Truth is the essence of life

. . . Happy are those who walk in it. (Buddhism)

1276. *Q*: I sense that the mystics possess an unfailing confidence. What is this solid foundation?

A: I possess the truth, and we shall see who will take it away. (Pascal)

1277. *Q*: If we are ready for an authentic teacher, will we find him? How does it happen?

A: Does a philosopher *seek* people to come and hear him? Does he not, rather, by his own nature, *attract* those who will be enriched by him? He is like the warming sun. What physician *seeks* for men to come and be healed? (Epictetus)

1278. *Q*: Apparently it is not easy to describe this new life which can be ours. What is the main difficulty?

A: That which is divine is invisible. (Philo)

1279. *Q*: How might a teacher attempt to describe it?

A: My life is like a stroll upon the beach. (Thoreau)

1280. *Q*: Suppose a man becomes conscious of his division into two contradictory selves — a right self and a wrong self. How can he recognize the worthy part, which he can then increase?

A: The precious, the living, the effectual part . . . is that of which he sees the reasonableness and excellence; that which approves itself to his intelligence, his conscience, his heart; that which answers to deep wants in his own soul, and of which he has the witness in his own inward and outward experience. (Channing)

1281. *Q*: Will you please remind us of our main aim — in other words, why are we working with these principles?

A: There is an endless Kingdom to be inhabited. (Bunyan)

1282. *Q*: If we read wise books with the wish to join ourselves with their higher facts, what response will the books
arouse in us?

A: The right feeling is, 'How strange this is! I never
thought of that before, and yet I see it is true.' (Ruskin)

1283. *Q*: May we have a truth which can arouse this feeling?

A: A man contains all that is needful to his government within himself. He is made a law unto himself. All real
good or evil that can befall him must be from himself . . . The
purpose of life seems to be to acquaint man with himself. He
is not to live to the future as described to him, but to live in
the real future by living to the real present. The highest
revelation is that God is in every man. (Emerson)

1284. *Q*: You have made us conscious of the inner call, but it
often fades away in the duties and confusions of the day.
Please remind us of its message.

A: Let us begin life anew. (Wallace)

Ponder these teachings of mysticism

a. Have a fondness for exploring the esoteric world.
b. The healing you need is always available.
c. Notice the refreshing honesty of these principles.
d. Increase your psychic sight, for it is everything.
e. To live rightly indicates cosmic wisdom.
f. Spiritual power commands all earthly power.
g. These teachings make us sensible and happy.
h. Influence yourself towards a richer life.
i. A lofty consciousness banishes self-conflict.
j. The true and free man is a law unto himself.

18. Mystic Good News for Your Daily Success

1285. *Q*: What is the good news of esoteric teachings?

A: You who suffer from the tribulations of life, you who have to struggle and endure, you who yearn for a life of truth, rejoice at the glad tidings! There is balm for the wounded, and there is bread for the hungry. There is water for the thirsty, and there is hope for the despairing. There is light for those in darkness, and there is inexhaustible blessing for the upright. (Buddhism)

1286. *Q*: Can we conclude that a spirit of authentic love will attract all that we truly need in life?

A: Those who come to seek truth with such a spirit of love and veneration, to them the Lord of Truth reveals the most wonderful things regarding Truth, Goodness, and Beauty. (Vivekananda)

1287. *Q*: I feel compelled to do so many things which are useless and boring. Need I submit to this mysterious pressure?

A: Nothing will protect us from external compulsion so much as the control of ourselves, and, as Seneca says, to submit yourself to reason is the way to make everything else submit to you. (Schopenhauer)

1288. *Q*: Interior control provides exterior control! What an astounding principle for us to grasp.

A: He who is firm in will moulds the world to himself. (Goethe)

1289. *Q:* Is it correct to say that a little light attracts more light, until we see life clearly?

A: You have found something of the truth of these testimonies upon you already, and more will immediately follow; for now, as you see, you are almost out of the wilderness. (Bunyan)

1290. *Q:* You have said we can use everything as an alarm clock for self-awakening. How can I use my dissatisfaction with myself?

A: Be dissatisfied with the life you are now leading, but when you have rejected it, do not be in despair over yourself . . . Learn what the wrestling teachers do. Has the boy fallen? 'Rise,' they say, 'and wrestle again until your strength is renewed.' That is how it should be with you. Realize that there is nothing more flexible than the human spirit. It needs but to *will,* and the thing is done; the spirit is set on the right path. (Epictetus)

1291. *Q:* There are times when I practise these fundamentals, yet see little difference in the way I feel or act. Perhaps I need some esoteric good news for those times.

A: If you have built castles in the air, your work need not be lost; that is where they should be. Now put the foundations under them. (Thoreau)

1292. *Q:* The mystics teach that the attainment of a superior psychic state makes everything right, including rightness with ourselves, with others, and with whatever life brings us. Please describe this superior state.

A: He who is one with himself, is everything. (Auerbach)

Good news about personal happiness

1293. *Q:* Apparently, as we advance inwardly, we change our minds as to what constitutes good news in worldly events.

A: In every epoch of the world, the great event, parent

of all others, is it not the arrival of a Thinker in the world? (Carlyle)

1294. Q: If we really want to know, will we eventually meet those who can teach us?

A: No one is so accursed by fate, no one is so utterly desolate, but some heart, though unknown, responds unto his own. (Longfellow)

1295. Q: One teacher stated that spiritual gold can be gained from an awakened man only after we have mined at least a bit of gold on our own. What did he mean?

A: A man can understand what is similar to something already existing in himself. (Amiel)

1296. Q: You have declared that we are *not* hopelessly trapped in life. That is enough good news to keep me vaulting forwards day and night.

A: Intellect annuls fate. So far as a man thinks, he is free. (Emerson)

1297. Q: Please show us how we can turn a negative experience into a positive force.

A: We owe a great debt to those who point out our faults for they humiliate us ... They prepare for us the exercise of correction and freedom from fault. (Pascal)

1298. Q: The members of our discussion group now understand some of the elementary principles of clear thinking, so may we have an advanced one?

A: How much confusion of thought comes from our interest in self, and from our vanity when thinking '*I* am so great' or '*I* have done this wonderful deed.' The thought of your ego stands between your rational nature and truth, banish it, and then you will see things as they are. He who thinks correctly will rid himself of ignorance and acquire wisdom. The ideas of 'I am' and 'I shall be' or 'I shall not be' do not occur to a clear thinker. (Buddha)

1299. Q: The need for surrendering our fictitious self is taught by every creed, but it arouses opposition within us, because we misunderstand its meaning. May we have a clarification?

A: For whilst in one sense we give up self to live the universal and absolute life of reason, yet that to which we thus surrender ourselves is in reality our truer self. The life of absolute truth or reason is not a life that is foreign to us. If it is above us, it is also within us. In yielding to it we are not submitting to an outward and arbitrary law or to an external authority, but to a law that has become our own law, an authority which has become enthroned in the inmost essence of our being. (Caird)

1300. Q: I know these teachings are true by the way they force me to look beyond my habitual self. At least I realize that rescue must come from a new and different source within myself.

A: As cold waters to a thirsty soul, so is good news from a far country. (Old Testament)

1301. Q: Please remind us of the need to *be* right, not merely to *appear* right.

A: Houses are built to live in, and not to look on. (Bacon)

Your relief from false guilt

1302. Q: I cannot accept any doctrine which excuses bad behaviour, but I love any teaching which shows us how to change our nature from bad to good. Esotericism shows the right way, which is why it is a truly moral teaching.

A: This is the way of happiness. (Plato)

1303. Q: I have been thinking of how we fall for the most obvious of lunacies, for example, trying to make people better by giving them material goods.

A: Human improvement is from within outwards. (Froude)

1304. *Q*: How can we get back to the healthy facts?

A: There is nothing more flattering than the bare truth, boldly uttered; but, all the same, those who can bear it are the rare exceptions in human nature. (Swetchine)

1305. *Q*: Why do we resist our healing medicine?

A: Truth is too simple for us; we do not like those who unmask our illusions. (Emerson)

1306. *Q*: I wonder whether I have drawn a correct conclusion from all this? Do we really owe nothing to a sick society except personal maturity and decency?

A: I do not give lectures or a little charity, when I give I give myself. (Whitman)

1307. *Q*: If only we could see this! What a relief from false guilt!

A: Who has hired you as a nurse to this sick society? (Tolstoy)

1308. *Q*: I am amazed at my first glimpse of a particular truth, which came as a faint flash, as you predicted it would. I am now starting to realize that the evil and cruelty of other people are, in reality, absolutely powerless to touch us.

A: Do they cast us out of the city? They cannot cast us out of that which is in the heavens. If they who hate us could do this, they would be doing something real against us. So long, however, as they cannot do this, they are but pelting us with drops of water or striking us with the wind. (Nazianzen)

1309. *Q*: It is delightful how the truth changes us! Since studying mystical teachings I have completely reversed my idea of what it means to be a great person.

A: The *happy* only are the truly *great*. (Young)

1310. *Q*: I have noticed that the more I study the more I want to study.

A: The criterion of true beauty is that it increases on examination; of false, that it lessens. (Greville)

1311. Q: I view esoteric teachings as a vast sea, upon which we must bravely dare the voyage. What is the good news for whoever sails all the way to the other side?

A: Nothing can trouble him more, nothing can move him, for he has cut all the thousand cords of will which hold us bound to the world . . . as desire, fear, envy, anger, drag us here and there in constant pain. He now looks back smiling and at rest on the delusions of the world, which once were able to move and agonize his spirit also. (Schopenhauer)

1312. Q: Can I personally achieve all this?

A: If self to self be true. (Calderon de la Barca)

Discover your inner miracle

1313. Q: Unless you have something to give other people, they seem cold and indifferent. I don't mean this as a complaint, but as a fact proven by personal experience. Obviously, only this new life of esoteric experience can deliver us from cold conditions.

A: Come near to this fire and you will soon be more than warm enough. (Terence)

1314. Q: But must we not give credit to society for trying to make it a warmer world through the administration of justice?

A: Love of justice in most men is only the fear of suffering from injustice. (La Rochefoucauld)

1315. Q: I have been helped enormously by hearing you say we must never be offended by the truth, no matter how badly it shakes our cherished beliefs about ourselves.

A: The courage of truth is the first qualification for philosophic studies. (Hegel)

1316. *Q*: I notice that the authentic mystics have nothing to do with sensational psychic events, which attract crowds, and which are often praised as miracles. They prefer to speak of the miracle of a changed inner life. Please comment.

A: Miracles are within us — natural facts which some call supernormal. (Balzac)

1317. *Q*: I think we all sense that an inner change to psychic health is all that really counts.

A: The only miracle that can truly be called a miracle. (Buddha)

1318. *Q*: A teacher stated that all forms of shame and disgrace are abolished through esoteric training. What did he mean?

A: What is natural is never disgraceful. (Euripides)

1319. *Q*: So often we find ourselves in the wrong place doing the wrong thing. I would like to know something about finding our rightful place in life.

A: A true man never frets about his place in the world, but just slides into it by the gravitation of his nature, and swings there as easily as a star. (Chapin)

1320. *Q*: With personal trueness we find ourselves where we should be, so now we must know how to become true.

A: Paradise is still in the world, but man is not in Paradise unless he is born again of God; in that case he stands in his new birth. (Boehme)

1321. *Q*: As I understand it, esotericism teaches two main points — man is enslaved, but can free himself. Will you review these?

A: We are free only so far as we are not dupes of ourselves, our pretexts, our instincts, our temperament. We are freed by energy and the critical spirit — that is to say, by detachment of soul, by self-government. So that we are enslaved, but susceptible of freedom; we are bound, but capable of shaking off our bonds. (Amiel)

How truth becomes your own truth

1322. *Q:* For more effective self-work, I would like to confirm a point. We hear the truth when it calls, but must then overcome our fault of hesitation, and answer the truth in the affirmative. Is that correct?

A: Man stands in strict connection with a higher fact never yet manifested. There is power over and behind us, and we are the channels of its communications ... This open channel to the highest life is the first and last reality, so subtle, so quiet, yet so tenacious, that although I have never expressed the truth, and although I have never heard the expression of it from any other, I know that the whole truth is here for me. (Emerson)

1323. *Q:* I have been remarkably stimulated by these ideas to ask questions I have never asked before. Perhaps this is a sign of self-awakening.

A: Inspiration must find answering inspiration. (Alcott)

1324. *Q:* May we have a helpful fact about self-transformation?

A: The man himself must become other than he was if he wants to comprehend truth — must become as true as truth itself. (Stirner)

1325. *Q:* From all we have heard, we need not make detailed plans for starting towards the richer life; we need only start whenever we like.

A: The hour is not past. Why will you put off your resolution? Arise, begin this very moment, and say, 'Now is the time to do: now is the time to fight, now is the proper time for amendment.' (Kempis)

1326. *Q:* I believe it is correct to say that the teachings of mysticism and esotericism are open to all who truly want self-liberty, to all who want to know for sure what life is all about.

A : It is the religion of universal inspiration. (Hinduism)

1327. *Q*: It is satisfying to know that these higher principles are available to all who really want them.

A : Like truths of science waiting to be caught. (Tennyson)

1328. *Q*: A group of us are now aware of how we were led down false spiritual paths, but also realize that our gullibility was our own fault. We want to *be* right,not *seem* right.

A : One ounce of the practice of righteousness and of spiritual self-realization outweighs tons and tons of frothy talk and nonsensical sentiments. Show us one, but one, gigantic spiritual genius growing out of all this dry dust of ignorance and fanaticism . . . open the windows of your hearts to the clear light of truth, and sit like children at the feet of those who know what they are talking about . . . Let us then listen attentively to what they say. (Vivekananda)

1329. *Q*: Please give us a message from their higher world.

A : With thinking we may be beside ourselves in a sane sense. By a conscious effort of the mind we can stand aloof from actions and their consequences, and all things, good and bad, go by us like a torrent. (Thoreau)

1330. *Q*: I am encouraged by realizing the existence of a few self-liberated individuals who can show us the way.

A : Really great minds seem to have . . . dissipated the clouds which concealed the heaven from our view, and they thus disclose to themselves and to us a clear and blissful world of everlasting repose. (Richter)

Accept this magnificent invitation

1331. *Q*: In discussing self-change with friends, I find that many of them are deeply discouraged over their faults. They feel that their hostilities and deceits are too deeply rooted to ever be pulled out and replaced with flowers.

A: Never let us be discouraged with ourselves. It is not when we are conscious of our faults that we are the most wicked, on the contrary, we are less so. We see by a brighter light, and let us remember for our consolation, that we never perceive our sins till we begin to cure them. (Fénelon)

1332. *Q*: What common weakness is removed by self-exploration?

A: Individual character is in the right that is in strict consistence with itself. Self-contradiction is the only wrong. (Schiller)

1333. *Q*: Then absence of self-contradiction means the presence of mental prosperity and genuine goodness?

A: Virtue is, like health, the harmony of the whole man. (Carlyle)

1334. *Q*: Then psychic health includes insight into the individual mind — its motives, its aspirations, its powers.

A: Who knows the mind has the key to all things else. (Alcott)

1335. *Q*: What is an example of a self-harming goal in a man?

A: To be recognized by the world for that which he had chosen as his idea of himself . . . recognizing him as the genius he must contrive to believe himself. (MacDonald)

1336. *Q*: The mystics say we have given ourselves false identities, that we tensely live from memorized selves, from which we must free ourselves. Please explain this.

A: I call that mind free which resists bondage of habit, which does not mechanically repeat itself and copy the past, which does not live on its old virtues, which does not enslave itself to precise rules, but which forgets what is behind, listens for new and higher monitions of conscience, and rejoices to pour itself forth in fresh and higher exertions. (Channing)

1337. *Q:* Your teachings have freed me from the strain and the folly of trying to imitate goodness. I now see the difference between *acting* good and *being* good.

A: Rejoice in being yourself a beautiful work of nature, and help yourself to further growth; that's the best thing. (Auerbach)

1338. *Q:* I think I finally see where we go wrong in our spiritual building. We try to compromise, we try to build a castle on ground which is at present occupied by a haunted house, which is an impossible task. Am I correct in believing that our first task is to clear the ground by giving up our precious nonsense?

A: Every step so downward, is a step upward. The man who renounces himself, comes to himself. (Emerson)

1339. *Q:* What does it mean to come to ourselves?

A: There arises in us the dawn of a Knowledge of Truth. (Lotze)

1340. *Q:* A new realization has come to me. The invitations we receive from surrounding society have some kind of a hidden price tag on them. But esotericism's invitation asks only that we receive what is truly right for us.

A: Come in! I will show thee that which will be profitable to thee. (Bunyan)

Be a student of esoteric facts

1341. *Q:* Members of our esoteric study group realize that truth alone is valuable, regardless of how it differs from our habitual ideas. Last night we discussed the pitiful thing which society calls friendship, which is really not much more than scared people huddling together against a threatening world.

A: I have found that no exertion of the legs can bring two minds much nearer to one another. (Thoreau)

1342. *Q:* I am confident that the esoteric path is the only way to rise above the human nightmare, but so many people think it is too far beyond them.

A: It can nevertheless be found. (Spinoza)

1343. *Q*: Sensing this, I would like the boldness needed for success.

A: Man, if you are anything at all, strive to walk alone and hold communion with yourself, instead of hiding in the chorus of men. Think, look around, arouse yourself, so that you will know who you are! (Epictetus)

1344. *Q*: I am becoming conscious of the harm in seeking approval from other human beings, but wish a scientific explanation of this false desire.

A: If you let yourself be made out in the right by another, you must no less let yourself be made out in the wrong by him. If approval and reward come to you from another, you must also expect his disapproval and punishment. (Stirner)

1345. *Q*: How can we learn the difference between mere human opinion and universal truth? There must be a special sense by which we can separate truth from error.

A: As the great ocean has only one taste, the taste of salt, so my doctrine has only one flavour, the flavour of emancipation. (Buddha)

1346. *Q*: You said that self-change also changes our attitude towards men of truth, that we newly value those who disturb us by giving us the blunt but life-saving truth about ourselves. Will you review this?

A: Dear to us are those who love us . . . but dearer are those who reject us as unworthy, for they add another life: they build a heaven before us whereof we had not dreamed, and thereby supply to us new powers out of the recesses of the spirit, and urge us to new and unattempted performances. (Emerson)

1347. *Q*: Will you say something about right attitudes towards an idea we may find difficult to understand?

A: If you are a lover of instruction, you will be well instructed. (Isocrates)

1348. *Q*: What would be a favourable result of our studies?

A: There is unspeakable pleasure attending the life of a voluntary student. (Goldsmith)

1349. *Q*: My question is about future conditions. What feeling should we have towards them?

A: The mood of one who, seeing himself carried swiftly towards an event of mighty import, has nothing to do but wait — the mood in which philosophy vests an even-minded man with the utmost calm, and is ever so serviceable. (Wallace)

1350. *Q*: What encouraging thought can help us when we fall short of our inner aims?

A: Begin wholly afresh. (Jefferies)

A far richer life awaits you!

1351. *Q*: We are beginning to see the need for a constructive kind of self-influence, so will you please help us in this area?

A: I know of no more encouraging fact than the unquestionable ability of a man to elevate his life by a conscious endeavour. It is something to be able to paint a particular picture, or to carve a statue, and so to make a few objects beautiful; but it is far more glorious to carve and paint the very atmosphere and medium through which we look, which morally we can do. To affect the quality of the day, that is the highest of art. (Thoreau)

1352. *Q*: We are told that goodness is its own reward, which I never used to believe, but now I am beginning to understand what it means.

A: What is virtue but repose of mind? (Thomson)

1353. *Q*: May we have a general rule for beneficial action?

A: Nothing leads to good which is not natural. (Schiller)

1354. *Q*: I have recently solved an esoteric mystery. I now see that what is truly right for me is also truly right for everyone else. My false guilt about my duties towards others has fallen away.

A: That is good news. (Bunyan)

1355. *Q*: These teachings reveal how we exhaust ourselves in useless tasks, like trying to impress others. Please tell us about a truly worthwhile task.

A: The decrease of the general cause of suffering — illusion — is the only pleasant work which lies before a man, and gives him that true happiness in which his life consists. (Tolstoy)

1356. *Q*: Is it really true that a sudden flash of insight can instantly banish all misery and reveal perfect peace? It sounds too wonderful!

A: Do you wish always to stray further? See, good lies as near; learn only to grasp happiness, for happiness is always here. (Goethe)

1357. *Q*: The mystics speak of the first dawning of understanding which comes to the sincere seeker. Will you please discuss it?

A: This sentiment is divine and deifying. It is the beatitude of man. It makes him illimitable. Through it, the soul first knows itself. It corrects the capital mistake of the infant man, who seeks to be great by following the great, and hopes to derive advantages *from another* — by showing the fountain of all good to be in himself, and that he, equally with every man, is an inlet into the deeps of Reason . . . then, deep melodies wander through his soul from Supreme Wisdom. (Emerson)

1358. Q: You are saying that if a man will only take care of his garden he cannot fail to see the flowers.

A: All is right with him. *(Theologia Germanica)*

1359. Q: How does a truth understood by the mind become a truth understood by the whole man?

A: Like a dreamer who, in the midst of a well-known and ordinary landscape, comes without warning upon the mighty cone of a mountain. (MacDonald)

1360. Q: Please supply a supreme principle for constant guidance and encouragement.

A: Higher, deeper, innermost, abides Another Life. *(Bhagavad-Gita)*

Good news that remains good news

a. Authentic love attracts all that you really need.
b. We should cheerfully give up a false sense of self.
c. Esotericism is a genuinely moral and sensible teaching.
d. A changed inner life is a true miracle!
e. You were made to be free from all unhappiness.
f. We must become as true as truth itself.
g. Accept the invitation of mysticism to trueness.
h. Be a loyal student of these higher principles.
i. Working for self-liberation is pleasant work.
j. Good news about yourself is now coming your way.

A Special Message for You

You are now on the interesting adventure of self-elevation. You are doing what is right, for it is this journey which gives a new and fresh meaning to life.

How do we rise above ourselves? If a man will only listen to the truth with a quiet mind, he will hear an inspiring message — the message of lasting happiness and authentic freedom. Out of these hundreds of questions and answers, I have selected twenty-five which shine with special brightness. Each has a unique power to reveal a higher place for you, so give them your glad attention: 7, 52, 78, 123, 174, 354, 466, 494, 852, 919, 935, 953, 986, 1078, 1119, 1156, 1172, 1198, 1200, 1254, 1269, 1275, 1299, 1325, 1351.

How can you find this New Life? There *is* a way. And you are now on that way. Walk on!

VERNON HOWARD

AUTHOR AND SOURCE INDEX

Author and Source Index

This index can aid you in the programmes listed in the front of the book. Let is also serve other methods of self-advancement, for example, you may wish to read everything by a particular author. The numbers refer to individual questions.

About Vernon Howard

For many years Vernon Howard has written and lectured on the one grand topic: "There is a way out of the human problem and any earnest person can find it." More than seven million readers have experienced the power of Mr. Howard's books, including translations into many languages. Vernon Howard's clear insight into human problems and his practical solutions attract thousands of new readers every year.

Groups of men and women who study Vernon Howard's teachings are located throughout the United States and Canada. The classes study Mr. Howard's books and listen to his taped lectures. Those who wish information on these meetings can write to New Life, PO Box 2230, Pine, Arizona 85544.

Please send us
the names and addresses of friends
who may be interested in these teachings.